THE TAO OF
MAYBE

Happiness. No Matter What.

Edition 1.2

by Shelli Wright

and Dr. Katherine Boutry

"Maybe the journey isn't about becoming anything. Maybe it's about unbecoming everything that isn't really you, so that you can be who you were meant to be in the first place."

~ Paulo Coelho (The Alchemist)

For my children, Graham and Hudson… and for yours.

~ Shelli

For Max, Penelope, Lily and Tom. Thank you for always providing me deep conversations. I love you.

~ Katherine

Tao /dou/

[Considered untranslatable, the exact meaning of "tao" remains elusive].

noun - the way; the path; both yin and yang, light and dark; in harmony with the natural order; the absolute principle underlying the universe; the flow of life.

Maybe /mābē/

adverb - possibly, perhaps

THE TAO OF MAYBE

Table of Contents

Introduction

This all started with two writers, a two hour weekly carpool commute and one very old story.

We were two moms and working professionals, feeling the same general unhappiness and stress that most Americans (and most humans) do. Katherine was in the throes of ending her 20-year marriage, and I was wallowing in a lackluster career and the difficulties of single parenthood. We were both always struggling with something. And we noticed that even though, each week we'd solve an issue and feel good about it, the next week there was a new issue or backpedaling of last week's resolve. It became clear it was an endless loop and we were exhausted by the cycle. We wanted out.

Then I got a random invite to a Kabbalah workshop. I wasn't then, or now, a member, but I'm always curious about the way people form beliefs. So there I was on a quiet Tuesday night as the speaker recited the Maybe parable. It sent my mind wandering down tangent paths so deeply, that I had to leave the workshop to go home to write my thoughts.

When I shared my experience with Kathy, she said, "you have to write this book." We quickly realized that we could use the modern science of neuroplasticity to turn this 2000-year-old wisdom into a way of life. This path has worked for us to change our neural pathways that create stress and unproductive beliefs. And we believe it can work for you.

The only obstacle is WANTING to let go of your nagging thoughts. It's simple but difficult. There are (at least) two things that work against us:

1) Fear: The mere act of *wanting* something poses a risk of failure or rejection. Ask any entertainment exec or Wall Street investor. "No" is safe. "Yes" is a risky proposition.

2) Habit: We've had these recurring thoughts so long, they're literally imprinted on our brains. Our mental computers are continuously running old programs in the background. To change the program requires defragmenting (more about that in a bit).

We've all had a friend who knows they should leave a bad relationship or job, but doesn't. Some of us have *been* that friend. It's easier to stay in a bad, but familiar situation, than to struggle free of it. Change can be hard. We sometimes stay in a state of sadness or disappointment just because it is familiar and comfortable. We tend to live out the same patterns over and over because it's easiest. And doing the same things over and over reinforces the same thoughts, which in turn, makes it more likely we'll keep living out those same patterns. By default, we keep running the same program on a loop.

A friend adopted a nine-year-old girl from a background of abuse and drug-addiction with a birth mother who was constantly in and out of rehab and court. The new adoptive mom was loving and calm, creating a peaceful, caring home life where the girl flourished. But the school kept calling about the girl's disruptions. This young girl had only ever known drama and so she was creating drama where none existed because that dynamic was familiar. It was safer for her brain to live with drama than to risk the unknown.

Change your habits, change your thoughts, change your mind.

This book was written for people living busy lives seeking a more relaxed state of mind. Inner peace is not to be confused with fleeting moments of joy or relaxation in an otherwise stressful life ... it's a sustained state of contentment with only fleeting moments of stress, worry or fear.

You probably know someone, or *of* someone, who embodies this way of being. Happenings roll off their backs, and they're seldom rattled or reactionary. They may be neither successful nor failed. Life just seems easier for them, or at least they are more *at ease* with it.

This state of Nirvana - this thing Zen masters seek - is often seen as a lifetime's pursuit by people in robes spending years in Nepal, months of silent *Vipassana*, or a diet of broth and yoga until they forget what it feels like to be burdened by a life of schedules and traffic.

That path simply isn't realistic or practical for those of us showing up for work, getting kids to their speech and debate team, and making a DMV appointment. Most of us have decided that kind of inner peace isn't possible for us. Who has time, actual time, for enlightenment?

You do.

You had time today in the car, in between phone calls, or in line at the check out. You'll have even more while lying in bed tonight. Achieving peace doesn't come from getting away from the stressors of every day life. It can happen amid, and despite, those stressors.

The Tao of Maybe is a tangible way to find inner peace in a hectic, modern world through the practice of non-attachment to preference.

Some of what you're about to read may sound counterintuitive to the principles of manifestation at first. But to be clear - these ideas and the Laws of Attraction are <u>not</u> mutually exclusive. In fact Katherine has several personal manifestation stories. For example, "I expressed, with no plan, that I wanted to visit Africa. Within 24 hours, I was offered a fantastic writing job that required me to stay in Côte d'Ivoire and South Africa. Note: I had no plan for how I would visit Africa. Also note: I got malaria, so manifestation doesn't mean perfection. And the world doesn't always manifest my desires in the *way* I plan. But as a collector of experiences, I'm happy to have had the whole range."

Be ready to change your mind.

By freeing ourselves from the tunnel vision of trying to manifest something specific, we open up to receiving things we couldn't possibly consider.

The Tao of Maybe is staying open and curious, especially and exactly when we most want to cling to fear. It explores:

- How hope becomes your prison
- How we get stuck in our own heads and the science behind it
- What we can do to change our thinking
- How to let go of preference for outcome
- How to seek neutral, rather than good or ba
- How to embrace the eternal now, rather than an uncertain future

A note on writing in the first person:

Two of us created this book, very much in collaboration. For simplicity's sake, I, Shelli will act as our first person narrator.

"EVENTUALLY YOU WILL SEE THAT THE
REAL CAUSE OF PROBLEMS IS NOT LIFE
ITSELF. IT'S THE COMMOTION THE
MIND MAKES ABOUT LIFE THAT REALLY
CAUSES THE PROBLEMS."

~ Michael Singer

Chapter 1. The Maybe Parable

———————————————

A poor farmer was struggling to make ends meet running his farm. He was blessed with a large tract of land, and he and his teenage son were doing their best to cultivate the acreage with one horse. Then one day, his horse took ill and died.

"What terrible news, how unlucky!" his friends and neighbors all exclaimed, as they watched the farmer and his boy bury the poor animal.

To which the farmer replied, "Maybe."

But only a few days later, a stranger traveling through town gifted him three horses!

"What good news! You're so lucky!" his friends and neighbors exclaimed, as they watched him take out two more old plows that had been gathering dust in a barn.

To which the farmer replied, "Maybe."

A few weeks later, the farmer and his son were tilling soil in corners of the land they didn't usually reach with just one horse, when they unwittingly rattled a hornets' nest. One of the horses got stung and reared up, kicking the son and badly breaking both his legs.

"What terrible news, how unlucky!" his friends and neighbors all exclaimed, as they watched the farmer craft a rolling chair for his maimed son.

To which the farmer replied, "Maybe."

A week later, a military convoy came knocking on doors, looking for able-bodied young men to go off to war to fight for their country, and very likely never come home. But the soldiers took one look at the wheelchair and left the farm without the son.

"What good news, you're so lucky!" his friends and neighbors shouted.

To which the farmer replied, "Maybe..."

That's all.

The simple, undeniable purity of the message suddenly and fundamentally shifted something for me. Instantly. Miraculously.

The point of the story isn't whether the farmer was lucky or unlucky (more on luck later). The point is that he chose not to come to a conclusion. Uncertainty is one of the hardest concepts for human beings to wrap their heads around. We want that uncomfortable feeling of the unknown to go away so badly, that we'd rather have any other answer than, 'I don't know.' Unarmed with certainty, we feel unable to act.

But this vulnerability is a strength rather than a weakness, and therein lies its power.

The only prerequisite for diving into this practice is that you be READY to let go of those thoughts you don't want. Ready to change your mind.

Sounds absurd - of course you're ready! But it's not as obvious as it seems. There are (at least) two things that keep us from letting go of our unwanted thoughts:

1) Fear: The mere act of *wanting* something poses a risk of failing. Ask any entertainment exec or Wall Street investor. "No" is safe. "Yes" is a risky proposition.

2) Habit: We've had our recurring thoughts so long, they're literally imprinted on our brains. Our mental computers are continuously running old programs in the background. To change the program requires defragmenting. More about that in a bit.

We've all had a friend who knows they should leave a bad relationship or job, but doesn't. We've *been* that friend. It's easier to stay in a bad, but familiar situation, than to struggle free of it. Change can be hard. We sometimes stay in a state of sadness or disappointment just because it's familiar and comfortable. We tend to live out the same patterns over and over because it's easiest. And doing the same things over and over reinforces the same thoughts, which in turn, makes it more likely we'll keep living out those same patterns. By default, we keep running the same program on a loop.

A woman adopted a nine-year-old girl from a background of abuse and drug-addiction with a birth mother who was constantly in and out of rehab and court. The new adoptive mom was loving and calm, creating a peaceful, caring home life where the girl flourished. But the school kept calling about the girl's disruptions. This young girl had only ever known drama and so she was creating drama where none existed because that dynamic was familiar. It was safer for her brain to live with drama than to risk the unknown.

Real happiness, i.e. inner peace, eludes the majority of us. Don't confuse happiness with fleeting moments of joyful or relaxed feelings in an otherwise stressful life. The inner peace we're talking about is a sustained state of contentment with only fleeting moments of stress, worry, and fear.

You probably know someone, or *of* someone, who embodies this way of being. Happenings roll off their backs, and they're seldom rattled or reactionary. They may be neither successful nor failed. Life just seems easier for them, or at least they are more *at ease* with it.

This state of Nirvana—this thing Zen masters seek—is often seen as a lifetime's pursuit by people in robes spending years in Nepal, months of silent *Vipassana,* or a diet of broth and yoga until they forget what it feels like to be burdened by a life of schedules and traffic.

That path simply isn't realistic or practical for those of us showing up for work, getting kids to their speech and debate team, and making a DMV appointment. Most of us have decided that kind of inner peace isn't possible for us. Who has time, actual time, for enlightenment?

You do.

You had time today in the car, in between phone calls, or in line at the check out. You'll have even more while lying in bed tonight. Achieving peace doesn't come from getting away from the stressors of every day life. It can happen amid, and despite, those stressors.

The Tao of Maybe is a tangible way to find inner peace in a hectic, modern world through the practice of non-attachment to preference.

Some of what you're about to read may sound counterintuitive to the principles of manifestation at first. But to be clear - The Tao of Maybe and the Laws of Attraction are not mutually exclusive. In fact, Katherine has a magical track record of manifestation experiences. For example, she expressed, with no plan, that she wanted to visit Africa. Within 24 hours, she was offered a fantastic writing job that required staying in Côte d'Ivoire and South Africa. Note: she had no plan for how she would visit Africa. Also note: she got malaria, so manifestation doesn't mean perfection. And the manifestation doesn't always happen in the *way* planned.

By freeing ourselves from the tunnel vision of trying to manifest something specific, we open up to receiving things we couldn't possibly consider.

The Tao of Maybe is staying open and curious, especially and exactly when we most want to cling to fear. Could happiness really be that simple and yet so profound?

Maybe.

"A FEELING OF AVERSION OR
ATTACHMENT TOWARD
SOMETHING IS YOUR CLUE THAT
THERE'S WORK TO BE DONE."

~ Ram Dass

Maybe Exercise 1: Commit and Observe

The beauty of this practice is that it costs nothing, requires no magic, no supplements, and no webinars. Just you and your willingness to unclench those butt cheeks. And all you have to do is commit to it.

The decision to do this often starts with an 'aha' moment (and many more along the way). Although it can be as simple as a flip of the switch, it requires reinforcement for it to stick. It is a "practice," which is hard at first and gets easier as you see the effects. It's two steps forward and one step back. But that step back can be a motivation killer, so it's important that you trust that it's worth it.

But just like sticking with yoga until you can finally bend your legs into lotus, here too, when you persist, you see progress.

Everything you think is created by you.

All your worry, stress, anger, annoyance, guilt, fear … IS MADE UP. You, and you alone, have created all the thoughts that bother you. And you continue to create them. They aren't pottery that was made and forever sits on a shelf— if you stop creating them, they don't exist any longer.

This is as simple as it is difficult. In order for any of this to work, you must accept it, otherwise you'll never stick with it. Even if you're not really sure you believe all this yet, just take a leap of faith. You have nothing to lose but your own negative thoughts.

Success is dependent on the trust and acceptance that you are in control of this process and you are the only obstacle in your way.

This also means you cannot get trapped in the blame game. Freedom from stress, anxiety, and want can only come from your own willingness. Blaming others, and the world around you for presenting stress, will only delay your ability to free yourself from it. It's not the rude driver, the impatient boss, or the forgetful spouse that gets your sympathetic nervous system engaged, it's your reaction to them. You must acknowledge that stress only comes from within.

You must believe it's possible to let go. We can, and must, decide to change our thoughts, and the first step is acknowledging them.

Your first assignment is simply to observe yourself. Notice your thoughts, where your stress comes from, when it happens, and how you feel.

Do not try to push it away, fix it, or even understand it. Just observe your own thoughts for the sake of being an observer. For the next few days make a mental (or literal) note when you feel distress. When thoughts of concern are persistent and affect your day, inspect it without judgment or conclusion. Just describe it for yourself.

Chapter 2. But Maybe Some People Are Just Lucky?

In the Maybe parable, is the farmer lucky for the gift of the horse? Is he unlucky for his son's injuries?

When this book was first conceived, the proposal made runner up in Hay House's publishing competition at the end of 2019. Subsequently, we had a book agent excited to bring us to market. Lucky?

Weeks later the pandemic of 2020 sidelined those publishing endeavors. Unlucky?

The next few years proved to be an incredible litmus test for our theory…

My Pandemic Luck

Up until the pandemic I was raising two kids and had a job, a boyfriend, a home, and a dog.

On Feb 28, 2020, my 60-hour-a-week job in event production for a 10,000-person conference in Vegas was canceled due to the pandemic: Three weeks before our event went live.

As my executive producer said, it was like being pregnant for nine months and not ever giving birth.

Of course, we'd all find out in a week or two that this was not an isolated story. The world was about to get Covid-canceled. And the ripples were coming.

The ripple for my career:

A complete flood. My industry was drowned underwater, not to return to its robust livelihood for years.

The ripple for my 15-year-old daughter:

School went online and her spring break flight to see her dad was canceled. The lull in June seemed like the safest window for her to fly across the country and spend the summer with him. And since school remained online in the fall, she stayed there for her junior year. And never returned.

The ripple for my 18-year-old son:

His part-time job vanished. He was already uninspired by community college, and now he had nothing. His days were filled with apathy, and by his 19th birthday, I realized he needed me to give him a nudge. My kick: if he wasn't going to be enrolled in school, he needed to find a job and start paying rent. He said, "Give me two months, and I'll move out." Two months later, he moved to Seattle.

The ripple for my home:

It was suddenly an empty nest. With both kids gone, I was lonely in a three-bedroom house, and didn't have the income to support it, so I decided to rent it out. Within 72 hours of posting to "see if anyone would bite," I had to move out.

The ripple for my dog:

Without a home, he became neurotic about moving around. He had been a runner since the day I saved him from being euthanized 10 years prior—I mean, he may have run away over 100 times—but since I lived in a development where everyone knew him, he always got returned. A week after leaving that home, he ran away for the last time.

The ripple for my love life:

My boyfriend and I were like a bird and a fish who fell in love at the water's edge but couldn't thrive in each other's worlds. After more than two years of failed compromises, the pandemic smooshed us together in a way that made it clear we were hurting each other. So I left.

Poof. I was suddenly and completely untethered.

But I wasn't devastated. Quite the contrary. I fully embraced the Maybe of it all and decided to trust in whatever was to come… to stay curious. I was excited to see where life would go. Since I had found renters so quickly, I only had time and space to take what I could fit in my car. With two small suitcases and two plastic bins, I downloaded some audio books and headed north. I visited friends, built fires at campsites, and car-camped at rest stops along the coast of California, Oregon, and Washington. I lived in a tent in a desert commune for a month, road tripped in an RV and visited my kids. I remained untethered for six months. And the unfolding of my nomadic life was spectacular.

Three years later…

My daughter thrived at online school and at her dad's place with a stepmom, stepbrothers, and pets. She went on to college for animation and our weekly video chats and multiple vacation visits were (and continue to be) richer than our passing conversations in the house or car. For 11 years, I'd been the homework parent, the chores parent, the doctor's appointment parent. Suddenly I got to be the vacation parent. As a bonus, I decided to shed the history of a bitter divorce. My ex and his wife and I finally put an ugly past behind us. We actually began laughing together again.

My son has created a whole life for himself in Seattle. He got a job within a few weeks (and a promotion shortly after), got his driver's license (which he couldn't conquer in L.A.), and his first girlfriend. We have such great chats and get along better than we did when he was under my roof. On my first visit, his girlfriend was eager to meet me, which says a lot about the way he portrays me, and that makes my insides smile.

Losing my job was actually a relief. Though I loved working for this agency/client before on some incredible jobs, this one was tedious and thankless and it was taking its toll on me. So, losing the stress and getting unemployment wasn't a bad thing at all.

My dog was found and adopted by an older couple whose dog had recently died. Though we'd given him a good home, he wasn't happy in an empty nest. Now he has a new home where he won't have to bounce around, and I'm happy for the three of them.

My boyfriend became my closest friend and we supported each other through the struggles of the pandemic and had fun along the way. We lived in a tent in the desert for a month, drove to Denver to pick up his new tiny home (The Traveling Stoop: a converted U-Haul truck) and drove through Washington, Colorado, New Mexico, Zion, the Valley of Fire, and so many other magical stops.

Friends I'd chatted with during the months kept asking what I was going to do when I got back to LA. 'Where are you going to live? What are you going to do for work?' They had genuine anxiety for me. I kept saying, "I don't know yet. But I'm sure it will present itself." I had a feeling I would discover what's next along my way.

A few weeks before my return to LA, I got a call from a friend. She needed to move into a family home for a bit and wanted a sublet to take over her room. Because her roommate was a mutual friend, I was the only logical choice. My next housing scenario was solved without me so much as looking at a listing.

The most unexpected cherry on top of all of this came just before arriving back in LA. I had no idea what I'd do for work.

Two days away from my home city, somewhere on a desert road in Joshua Tree, I got a call from a CEO/CTO team I'd worked for a decade prior. The CEO had read about my nomadic travels in an article I wrote for *Elephant Journal*. He particularly noticed that I was out of work. And it just so happened that they had a new company they needed some help with. So, without sending out a resume or upgrading my LinkedIn account, I had work. A six month freelance contract turned into two years of employment and stock options.

My letting go of attachment to what or how anything came about paved the way to a most wonderful journey.

Now, the less I try to plan out my future, the more excited I am about the possibilities.

Katherine's Pandemic Luck

"COVID hit us all unexpectedly. In many ways, it was the ultimate test of the Maybe thinking Shelli and I had been practicing. This felt like the final exam.

My ripples were less picturesque than Shelli's, but nevertheless meaningful. My adult children came home unexpectedly for a year and my youngest, coping with being the only kid home dealing with divorced parents, had her siblings back. I suddenly needed a house to fit everyone in again as my post-divorce, "only one child home," glamorous, but tiny, beach apartment wouldn't cut it. This was an unexpected opportunity for us to reconnect, and no way was I going to miss it.

So I did something I never thought I could. I bought a teardown house in a neighborhood I didn't know much about but could afford, and embarked on a renovation project I wasn't sure I could pull off. It required a lot of trust and Maybe moments, as well as a full-on learning curve, but in the end, we have a place that is perfect for us and the two COVID puppies we adopted who have brought us so much joy and would not have been possible if we weren't all working from home with a grassy yard.

I also had just started dating a new man in February 2020, right before the pandemic shut everything down. The jury was still out. He was different from any man I'd ever dated (which was actually good), but I had a lot of doubts that we would last because he was not the kind of guy I expected to like. Still, I kept wanting to see him. I had a lot of fun with him. He made me laugh and feel really good. I practiced Maybe thinking for the first time in a romantic relationship, and the results have been great. I stayed patient and curious rather than jumping to a hasty decision on "us" and "him" and our potential. And I am finally with a partner who really gets me and with whom everything feels natural and effortless. And we're getting married. Through the pandemic limiting both of our plans to date a lot and keep it light, I gave love a second chance. And I've learned so much about what's really important in a relationship at an age when I was starting to think I knew it all. So far from it. :)

Because this relationship has given me such a firm foundation of love and trust, and because there hasn't been the all-consuming drama of my previous dating life, I was able to explore healing with my parents and to identify where all that drama had been coming from before. Through working with a therapist, I learned that my mother—because of her own trauma—likely suffers from a personality disorder. This information has helped me to resolve decades of painful interactions that I had always thought were my fault, but for which I blamed her. Neither of those ideas were accurate. If Maybe teaches us anything, it is that our perspective can always change with additional information, and that if we stay open, there is so much personal growth and evolution possible in our own lives. Our stories are far from over, even if we have been telling them for years.

Through COVID, I also started working on a novel I had put aside because I was "too busy" and rediscovered both my love for that project and a new outlet for my creativity in the time I had previously used for commuting.

When I made peace with the fact that the creativity program I had envisioned and then created at my college appeared to be dead because the pandemic had shut down our activities and reduced enrollment, I converted the conference into a podcast series.

And most importantly, with my kids home, I was able to reconnect with all three of them and spend quality time I never would have had. I never imagined my older children would move home for a year again in my lifetime, and what a blessing it has been. While I do not in any way want to understate the pain so many have suffered as a result of COVID, I am grateful

for this beautiful life that keeps us guessing and for the peace
that Maybe has given me through constant change."

So how does luck factor into happiness? A British psychologist wanted to find out.

Dr. Richard Wiseman (*The Luck Factor*) conducted a 10-year study with a group of 400 volunteers, ages 18 - 84, who self-identified as either "lucky" or "unlucky."

The study had two goals:

1. To determine whether self-identified "lucky" people actually had an increased incidence of good fortune or if they just perceived themselves that way, and

2. (Spoiler alert) Since he found the latter was true, to figure out how one achieves the feeling of being lucky.

One of the most poignant examples came early on in the study. Dr. Wiseman had an interview with one of the self identified "lucky" participants, who came in wearing a cast from foot to hip.

Wiseman asked, "What happened?"

The man replied, "I fell down a flight of stairs."

"Wow. That's terrible."

The man looked at Wiseman in astonishment, "Are you kidding? I could have broken my neck!"

And there you have it. Whether he was lucky or unlucky is entirely beside the point. He sees his life as a series of good fortune no matter what happens. Luck - and happiness - is in the eye of the beholder.

Once this truth was evident, Dr. Wiseman set out to study the differences between lucky and unlucky people, in an effort to help teach people how to feel luckier.

He ran a series of tests, the "newspaper photos" being one of our favorites. He printed a simple two-page newspaper deck and asked all of the test subjects to tell him how many photos were in the newspaper.

On average, the unlucky people answered, "43 photos," in about 2-3 minutes. The lucky people answered, "43 photos," in about 20-30 seconds.

See, the very first headline read, "You can stop reading. There are 43 photos."

The unlucky people were so narrowly focused on counting, that they weren't open to anything else.

Some might think, so what? They were focused on a task. That's not a bad thing. How does that make someone unlucky in life? Well, imagine the following scenario: You're invited to a cocktail party where you know no one and, let's say, you're at a time in your life where you want to find someone special to settle down with. You're going to spend the evening scanning the faces in the room for a mate (counting the photos), and disregard everyone else (the headlines).

You are absolutely going to miss that person who might become a lifelong friend. Or the entrepreneur who is about to launch a startup and will have a great job to offer you in three months. Or that person who knew a friend of your mom who brings you down memory lane. Who knows? Well, actually, the lucky person knows because they ask. They listen. And they look. They focus on what's in front of them, in the present, staying curious, rather than critical.

"Whatever you believe,
you will find that you are correct.
The universe has a way of presenting
to you exactly what you believe. If you
think life is great, you are correct. If
you think life is tough, you will be
proven correct too."

~ Anita Moorjani

Maybe Exercise 2: Be Dirty Harry

"Do you feel lucky?"

We are not the first or last to say that feeling lucky requires a few simple things:

1. Take chances ("You lose 100% of the shots you don't take.")

2. Set positive goals.

3. Visualize good fortune.

4. Practice gratitude for even the smallest of positive events.

5. Look for the silver lining in otherwise negative outcomes.

There is a critical addition to all of the above. You have to do more than "believe" good things will happen; you have to "feel" what it would feel like when it happens.

Joe Dispenza is a big proponent of this, because ultimately the mind doesn't know the difference between the reality in your mind and the reality in the 3D world. So if you can imagine it's happened, your brain thinks it actually has.

Chapter 3. Enlightenment Isn't Just for Hippies.

Creation said, "I want to hide something from the humans until they are ready for it. It is the realization that they create their own reality."

Eagle said, "Give it to me. I will take it to the moon."

Creator said, "No. One day they will go there and find it."

Salmon said, I will take it to the bottom of the ocean."

Creator said, "No. They will go there, too."

Buffalo said, "I will bury it on the Great Plains."

Creator said, "They will cut into the skin of the earth and find it even there."

Grandmother who lives in the breast of Mother Earth,

and who has no physical eyes but sees with spiritual eyes, said,

"Put it inside of them."

And the Creator said, "It is done."

~ from the Hopi Nation

The sound bath and breathwork talk can sound like a luxury for the "love and light" crowd on Instagram.

But someone has to make the world go round, right? Isn't this hippy dippy stuff kind of frivolous?

Actually, It's a matter of life and death.

"Stress kills," according to multiple, global health organizations (*Psychology Today*). A large number of scientific studies (*The US National Library of Medicine, National Institute of Health and PubMed*) have identified stress as the major cause for a staggering increase in cancer, strokes, and heart attacks over the past few decades.

The biological purpose of the stress response—increased heart rate and blood pressure to help us fight or take flight—is not as necessary as when we were cave dwellers. Yet, in our modern day we perceive social, political, and financial threats every day. And that stress has become the number one killer of our time.

> *Excerpt from New Atlas Health and Well Being (June 19, 2018 edition):*
>
> *A massive Swedish study spanning 30 years of data examining over one million people has found a strong association between persons suffering from stress disorders (including PTSD) with an increased risk of developing autoimmune diseases such as arthritis and Crohn's disease. The striking results found that those suffering from a diagnosed stress-related disorder were 30 - 40% more likely to subsequently be diagnosed with one of 41 different autoimmune diseases.... including rheumatoid arthritis, psoriasis, and celiac disease.*

The link between traumatic life stresses and autoimmune disorders probably seems obvious. Some may think, I don't have PTSD, I just have regular every day stress. The thing is, suffering from something everyday makes it chronic, and that's just as debilitating. Most of us have experienced stress manifesting in physical symptoms, such as stomach aches, headaches, tense muscles, or jittery hands.

This state of threatened homeostasis provoked by a psychological, environmental, or physiological stressor (aka realizing you lost your phone, getting stuck in traffic when you're already late, or meeting a myriad of expectations) brings on multiple neurochemical and hormonal alterations by activating the sympathetic nervous system (SNS) and the hypothalamic-pituitary-adrenal (HPA) axis.

When stress stimuli are in control, the body responds in a physiological way: the nervous system axis is woken up to release chemical mediators to protect our body from stress (fight or flight mode). This state is beneficial to our survival and recovery. But when stress stimuli are prolonged, persistent or exaggerated, they chronically increase allostasis and lead to pathophysiology (in other words, bad health).

In the last few decades, accumulating evidence indicates that chronic (severe or prolonged) stress results in increased risk for physical and psychiatric disorders:

- cardiovascular diseases (i.e., hypertension and atherosclerosis),
- psychotic and neurodegenerative disorders (i.e. Alzheimer's and Parkinson's)
- metabolic diseases (i.e., diabetes and non-alcoholic fatty liver disease, NAFLD),

Fatty liver disease?! Jeez. We're not suggesting that drinking alcohol is healthy, but if you can get liver disease from stress, then relaxing with a glass of wine might be just what the doctor ordered.

The Heart and Soul Study looked into people's history of psychological stress, measured their inflammatory cytokines, and hypothesized a connection. Inflammatory cytokines are chemicals released by the immune system activating armies of cells to attack invaders such as viruses, pathogenic bacteria, or cancer. When our immune system is over-activated it can lead to autoimmune disease. Most modern chronic disease is associated with elevations in these cytokines.

> **75% - 90% of all human diseases are related to the activation of the stress system.**

What activates that system? We have thoughts like,

"I desperately need this."

"I'm afraid something bad is going to happen."

"What if I miss my flight?"

"What if things don't go well?"

These thoughts are the source of our anxiety. Not the events happening outside of us.

Because of this perceived stress, Americans are not the happiest of souls, and it has nothing to do with political, social or financial realities. In the history of the Harris Poll (which conducts annual happiness surveys of roughly 2,000 adult Americans), the highest happiness index we have achieved was

35% in 2008 and 2009, housing crisis be damned. That means at its best, 65% of the American sample population is dissatisfied and knows it. Gallup has been conducting an even larger annual study (2.5 million Americans) for the past decade. In his article "The Unhappy States of America," Richard Florida discusses the Gallup poll results: Even with the economy humming, Americans were feeling more anxious, depressed, and unhappy with their lives in 2018 than they were in 2009.

Our happiness, or what researchers refer to as "subjective well-being," is down across the nation... America these days is not a happy place. Polarization is at an all-time high, and a feeling of malaise, or worse, grips the nation.

And it's not just America (ranked 18th happiest out of over 150 countries). Even if you live in the happiest country on the planet, Finland (5 years running at the time of this publication according to *Gallup's World Happiness Report*), you're still 25% likely to be unhappy.

This nebulous malaise is what The Tao of Maybe seeks to alleviate. The happiness studies show us that external circumstances rarely cause our unhappiness. Rather, it is our thoughts and feelings about the present and our discomfort with uncertainty that make us miserable. Our endless unhappy thoughts are an epidemic, blind to age, race, or sexual orientation. We all do it - we worry too much.

As a society, convinced that we're not happy (or not happy enough), we hold our proverbial breath until "this" happens, or until we get "that." This desire for an outcome (usually over which we have little to no control) is the root of all suffering according to the Buddha. And it's these thoughts around want or lack that keep us stuck.

All of this is to say, we're unhappy AND unhealthy. The idea that we can deal with stress on the daily and take a vacation once every year or two to unwind isn't going to cut it.

But we have the power to change that.

Of course, there are proven ways to reduce stress that have positive effects on our health: meditation, sleep, drugs, exercise, and sex to name a few. They can provide immediate and temporary relief from our perceived problems, but they seldom help to achieve the permanent task of fixing our thinking. And when the temporary relief fades, we lower our expectations for happiness.

As we learn to redirect our thoughts internally, the outside circumstances have less and less influence on our emotional state.

In order for the life you want to unfold, your mind must step aside.

Practicing The Tao of Maybe is a commitment to accepting that your thoughts are a by-product of wanting to control your outside circumstances. And every obstacle to changing your thoughts… is you.

"WE MUST BE WILLING
TO LET GO OF THE LIFE WE'VE
PLANNED, SO AS TO HAVE THE LIFE
THAT IS WAITING FOR US."

~ Joseph Campbell

Maybe Exercise 3: Drive Yourself Uncrazy

Traffic.

One of the simplest examples of a stress-inducing part of our daily lives is driving. If you live anywhere with remotely as much traffic as LA like we do, you've had the maddening experience of being stuck in traffic. You'll never make it to your destination on time. You're angry at the driver ahead of you. Annoyed by the driver next to you. You start to panic. Your heart races, your face maybe starts getting hot. Your stress response is in full effect.

Hit pause. Notice what your body is doing. Have you been craning your neck? Are your hands tight on the wheel? Are your shoulders up to your ears? Stop changing lanes. Stop the panic. Take a breath.

Now consider your reality. You probably will be late. Someone might be upset with you. Is there anything you can do about it? Is there a better route… can you call a friend to pick up your kids… or a co-worker to stall the meeting?

Take reasonable actions but not knee-jerk reactions. You might not be that late. And who's to say the slow-moving traffic isn't actually beneficial? Maybe the extra few minutes allows you to hear an important radio interview, or to remember to call your mother, or perhaps even to avert a possible accident you would have encountered had you arrived at your destination more quickly. It doesn't matter if these better-feeling alternatives are true or not. What matters is that they stop you from increasing your stress.

Admit to yourself, "I'm already late. Being upset, angry, and stressed about being late, won't make me any less late." It will only increase the chances that your actions may make things worse, such as causing you to get a speeding ticket or have an accident.

Since stress is the most widely recognized enemy to human health, you're actually compromising your health by focusing on things you cannot control anyway.

Consider that you now have a little extra time in the car. Listen to the podcast your friend sent a week ago. Call your sister. Dictate an email on your (hands free) phone to save time writing it later. Hey, look at that, you've just balanced out the time you lost. Becoming productive in that time helps let go of the stress.

If you're saying, "No way. That's not going to work." Or, "Sure, I can try that," but then the first time you try, you fail miserably... don't give up.

We asked you to accept this truth and commit to the practice for a reason - it's not second nature. You're going to hit road blocks (pun intended). But you can get through them and you're going to get better at it.

Chapter 4. Hope is a Four Letter Word

Success is as dangerous as failure. Hope is as hollow as fear.
~ Lao Tzu, Tao Te Ching

The Hope Holding Tank

The word, "hope" is tricky. For most, it inspires loving, positive thoughts. So the suggestion that hope can be making you unhappy makes most people stop in their tracks (including Kathy, at first).

In fact, this book almost didn't get written because we disagreed about hope. When I told Kathy that one of the pivotal tenets of the Tao of Maybe was that "hope was a four-letter word," she told me that maybe we couldn't write this book together. She started putting her notebook away and capping her pen. But you're reading this book, which means she changed her mind.

Katherine's View on Hope…

"To say I was originally resistant to vilifying hope is an understatement. I was upset that anyone would dis hope; the one thing that had single-handedly kept me going through a tough childhood, an uneven career as a TV writer, and then an unhappy marriage. I didn't want any part of that cynical view. But because I trusted Shelli, I decided to hear her out. And that trust paid off. When I examined how hope had functioned in my own life, I had an epiphany or two. Maybe hope had made me feel a whole lot better in tough moments, but it had also kept me from breaking away from situations and people I should have ditched long before. I was attached at the hip to hope because it had gotten me through a lot of difficult times.

Hope keeps us stuck in what I call "the hope holding tank." For me, it held the promise that things would get better, that people in my life would change. It relied on the denial and wishful thinking that one day, my disengaged parents would see what a great kid they had, spin on their heels, and carry me on their shoulders in tearful recognition. In the same way, I imagined that if I cooked well, was an excellent mother, never refused sex, and knocked myself out with two full-time jobs in academia at the same time, THEN I would be rewarded with love and affection. Big fat nope. Instead, I spent forty years fantasizing about the day when things would magically get better.

Hope acts like a mask, and it's temporary. The ache comes back.

Hope kept me focused on the future, rather than allowing me to face the reality of the present: that my marriage had problems. Newsflash: if a situation or person feels bad in the beginning, hope isn't going to change that. If I had trusted that the universe would support me instead of hoping things would change, I would have made the necessary adjustments to my life a lot sooner.

When I was a senior in high school, I was a "good girl" as the daughters of mothers with borderline personality disorder often are—valedictorian of my class, honors in everything, published in Time magazine, president of multiple clubs, Governor's School of the Sciences Scholar, National Merit Scholar, and NJ Scholar's Program participant, etc. I was exhausting in my pursuit of labels that would finally prove I was worthy. The problem was that they never gave me that feeling of lovability I was searching for. Disappointed, I set my sights on the hardest thing I could think of: to go to Harvard. I only applied to two other schools because I was so sure I was meant to get in. Long story short, I ripped open that suspiciously thin envelope thinking that Harvard must send all the info about move-in day by white-gloved private messenger, only to discover— not only did I not get in, I didn't even get waitlisted. What made it slightly worse was that based on the strength of my conviction, my high school boyfriend had only applied to schools in Boston so that we could be together. I was completely devastated the way only a 17-year-old can be. My whole life was "ruined" both professionally and romantically.

In hindsight, I know it was absolutely the best outcome for my life. Number one, I clearly needed to understand that my achievements didn't make me lovable (only being a loving and compassionate human being can do that). Number two, that boyfriend really needed to be several states away so that we could realize we were really different people. And number three, if I had gone as an undergraduate, I would have missed out on the amazing mentors and experiences I had in the school I did attend, and would likely not have later been accepted to Harvard as a graduate student.

It's important to feel our disappointment, but not be paralyzed by it, to trust the Universe.

I appreciated getting into Harvard so much more when it finally happened, and was a much more mature person when I got there. Had I gotten in right away, I would not have brought my A-game, and would have wasted the opportunity. I needed that time to mature as a scholar and as a person. I would tell my 17-year-old self (and tell every anxious teen I know applying to college) that we should not become rigidly attached to an outcome, but rather trust that the Universe always sends us what we need."

The Hope Band Aid

Hope does serve a useful purpose. Just as a Band-Aid stops the bleeding and protects delicate cuts from bacteria in order to heal, hope can protect you from psychological trauma.

When I got the call from my mom from her office in the Twin Towers on the morning of 9/11 to tell me she was getting out of the building, hope was the psychological self-preservation mechanism I needed to survive.

She had called to say her tower wasn't the one hit, but we were still on the phone when the second plane crashed into her building, several floors below. The sound was horrific, but she was still on the line and said she'd call me as soon as she got out. I would never get that call.

When I saw her tower crumble on tv, I knew in my body that she did not make it out. It wasn't a logical feeling, just a knowing.

But accepting that in the moment would have undone me, and I wouldn't have been able to function or to take care of my 10-week old son.

I hoped that I was wrong. I hoped that phones were just out of order. I hoped that she was trapped in a pocket of rubble in the Path station, eating Snickers and drinking Evian until the rescuers could find her and she'd crack jokes with them. I even hoped that she was in a hospital with amnesia or some other soap opera storyline logic.

That hope helped me get through the day. And the next day, and the next. It helped me sit up long enough to breastfeed my infant.

As the days went on, the hope got more unrealistic, more fantastical, and it became harder and harder to live in denial. After two weeks, I finally made the choice to give up hope and take steps toward reality. I made memorial service arrangements and began the forward progression of grieving.

Was hope useful at first? Yes. It was my brain's very necessary tool to protect me from crippling pain. Was it useful two weeks later? No. It was delusional. And it was keeping me stuck. To move on, I had to let go of the hope that was holding me back.

Hope can save us from despair when we feel like giving up or just provide everyday motivation. It's optimism and sunshine when it's pouring buckets, and it makes us feel good to think about happy things. That's all true. Everyday hope offers the possibility of "better."

But the unspoken end of that sentence is, better… than where we are now. Hope inherently implies that there is something wrong or lacking with what we have. And that makes it a trap, for two reasons:

1. Hope is always about the future and what is currently out of reach.

Because hope, by definition, relates to the future, it keeps us from living in the now. Think about it... can you hope for something that is already happening? No. It may (or may not) exist soon, but it does not exist yet. It will always be the near, the almost, the not yet... but never the now. So, hope is fantasizing about what doesn't exist. Improving our life circumstances requires seeing clearly and being uncomfortable enough with what's not working that we are willing to make a change. The first step to living a contented life is accepting what is now as if that is all there will ever be.

2. Being attached to a specific hope narrows our chances for happiness.

Hoping for a specific outcome can be a set-up for disappointment. If there is only a narrow result that we consider a win, that means all the other possible outcomes are categorized as a fail.

A writer friend wanted very much to get signed with literary managers, and was elated with that win when it happened, only to dissolve the relationship after a year of getting nowhere. The win was a dud. During the same time period, a producer they met quite accidentally at a cocktail party brought several work opportunities that sent them to international locations. The fulfilled hope of getting a manager was disappointing, while the unexpected surprises of the Universe were delightful.

Does this mean being a pessimist is more realistic? On the contrary. The opposite of hope isn't despair; it's trust.

Sometimes the Universe truly serves us up a shit biscuit and we feel awful. We lose a job. Our spouse is having an affair. Our kid failed half of his classes and now won't get into college. It's true that we aren't going to like everything that happens at all times. But if we remain open to the experience and allow for different outcomes, we eliminate a lot of agony. The less preference we have for the specifics of the future, the more room we make to be content. The goal isn't to feel good or bad about a circumstance, it's to be neutral, non-reactive, and open to the lesson and the healing in every experience.

If the opposite of hope is trust, how do we trust through difficult times? The answer is: stay neutral and be curious.

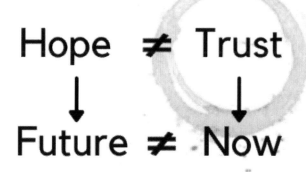

Hope ≠ Trust

↓   ↓

Future ≠ Now

1. Stay Neutral.

Life has its ups and downs. Embracing the Tao of Maybe won't change the fact that things aren't always going to go the way we'd like. It's reasonable to get upset, angry, or sad about events for a brief period of time. But it's counterproductive to let it be a lasting or repetitive thought process. It serves us better to accept the event and move on. When we trust that in the bigger scheme of things, each experience is one we are meant to have, and that the Universe (or God) guides us to the path of personal growth, we can stop clinging to our sense of imagined control. There is almost always a lesson in life's events, and if we refuse to learn it, it gets served right back up on a hot steaming plate until we do.

2. Be Curious.

Life is going to unfold in front of you no matter what you do, no matter how you feel about it. It is not a thing to be controlled, but to be experienced.

If we trust that everything happening right now needs to happen to lead to what happens next, (and that what happens next is also necessary), we free ourselves from the prison of hope and the illusion of control. We allow ourselves to experience more joy and positivity right NOW, by simply letting go of attachment to preference. There is a delicious relief in giving our worries to the Universe.

We're not suggesting to give up plans and precautions. Imagine being a passenger on a motorcycle. You can either squeeze your butt cheeks and refuse to look at the scenery, or surrender and enjoy the ride. Neither choice affects the outcome. In fact, being overly nervous might cause you to distract the driver. We're not saying don't plan—you should wear a helmet and protective gear, make sure the driver is experienced and cautious, and learn how to lean with the bike. But your choice of emotional reaction affects your experience A LOT. Those niggling thoughts won't make danger less likely, but they will ruin your enjoyment.

Obsessively worrying about something that might happen in the future doesn't bring you relief and it doesn't control the outcome. For example, let's say Peter takes an exam. He feels some anxiety while waiting to get the results. One moment he feels hopeful: "I think I did well, but I won't be able to celebrate until I see the results." One moment, he feels doubtful: "I think I bombed, and I'm dreading seeing my grade." He checks online several times a day looking to see if the scores have been posted yet. He crosses his fingers, prays, and even holds his breath as he finally reads the results. The reality is, the test is already done. The score already exists. None of the thoughts between the exam and the score have any bearing on it. The doomsday thoughts and discomfort only diminished his ability to feel content in the moment. (Not to mention the fact that failing Organic Chemistry might save you from going to medical school and embarking on the wrong career in an effort to please your parents.) After the initial shock, you might feel enormous relief and the freedom to pursue your passion. (Just sayin' …that happened to Kathy).

Instead, take necessary actions, and then surrender to the Universe's plan.

Hope is a wolf in sheep's clothing. It tells us that we will be happy when ___(fill in the blank)___ happens. Hope says, "I'm not at my happiest now, but I could be happier in the future."

In a way, hope is an act of violence against the present moment.

FEAR AND TRUST
BOTH DEMAND THAT YOU BELIEVE
IN SOMETHING THAT HAS NOT
HAPPENED.

Maybe Exercise 4: Act Like a Child

If you research existing methods for fostering curiosity, 99% of what you'll find is aimed at children. We're so programmed to think wonder is a childish trait, that we don't reward adults for asking questions. We're supposed to know, or find out an answer, rather than having a playful curiosity about the ambiguous nature of our existence.

Yet, in a 2004 study on happiness, curiosity was found to be one of the top 5 out of 24 strengths that increases happiness. (Christopher Peterson & Martin Seligman, (2004). *Character Strengths and Virtues: A Handbook and Classification.*)

This week, practice thinking like a kid again. Instead of taking everyday life at face value, question everything. You feel hungry… "Am I actually hungry or am I anxious, or bored?"

You feel irritated about a friend who's late for lunch… "I wonder if they'll have an interesting story about why they're late, or if it's just traffic." Or "I wonder how many passersby I can get to smile at me as I wait."

You're feeling awkward about being alone in a room full of people… Play the story game about a few of the people's lives: "that one just moved back from Europe for a new job. That one had a bitter divorce and is taking Tai Chi."

You see a house for sale and know that it's too expensive for you... imagine what would have to happen for you to buy that house. You befriend the owner and strike an incredible deal, you get a lump sum from a great aunt that you didn't know was coming.

You take a bite of a delicious or terrible meal... "What gives it that flavor? How many of the ingredients can I identify?"

Play a game of 20 questions or I spy with your friend while you're driving or having coffee.

When a friend tells you something ordinary like, "the kids and I are going to the beach this weekend," ask a question about it... "Who do you think loves the beach most out of all of you? What's your favorite thing to do while you're there?" Dive deeper into mundane conversations.

You see a tall building,... "I wonder how many floors it has? What year was it built? What or who is inside?"

Advanced: When you have an impending life event that you hope will go a certain way (i.e. you apply for a job, have a second date with a cute woman you're interested in, see an apartment you'd really like), imagine it goes the other way, but imagine it with neutrality. Find ways that it could be a good thing. What could it lead to next?

Chapter 5. Jumping Into the Unknown

To conquer the unknown you must trust.

~ Yogi Bhajan

Uncertainty (whether it be fear or hope) creates anxiety. Consider these examples…

Imagine you're on a job interview. You prepare, you dress appropriately, you get a good night's sleep and you do your best. You shake hands and leave. You hear nothing for days. You send an email. They respond that they're still interviewing candidates. Waiting is stressing you out. Your life is on hold. Then you hear. You didn't get the job. Your shoulders droop a little. You exhale. You're not happy about it.

You feel pretty down for a day or three. But there is relief that the anxiety of the unknown is finally over.

What if you could experience that relief before hearing the answer? All the time, in fact? You can: by letting go of preference. Decide that you are legitimately at peace with the unknown, not just faking it; you are truly okay with not knowing the outcome. That is power because you control your state of mind—not the employer, not the date who ghosted you, not the landlord. You.

An extreme example of this comes in the form of parents living the nightmare of having a missing child. A UK study of 12 families of missing children noted "The emotional impact is significant." The term "living in limbo" is often used to describe how families are unable to move on while a loved one is missing, as they fluctuate between hope and hopelessness.

Families in that dreadful limbo can't work or take care of the house or eat or engage with people, because that terrible question hangs over their lives. Eventually, living in that awful unknown leads to a desire to end the suffering. To be released.

Parents and siblings of missing children have high incidents of suicide, divorce, drug use and depression. Psychologists call this 'ambiguous loss.'

"When a missing child is found dead, hopefulness ends —but so does a period of ambiguity about the child's fate. The loss is resolved and becomes absolute. Established rituals of mourning can then take place. Closure is possible."

Finding out the worst has happened can come as a tragic relief because hope—ping ponging between being wildly hopeful and desperately hopeless—causes agony.

Here's a test… Say you're saving up for a vacation. Take a look at the graphic. This is what you saved!

$0 $4,000

How do you feel about it? Pretty good, right?

But this is what you hoped to save:

$0 $4,000 $5,000

$4,000 of $5,000

Now, how do you feel? Probably not as good as with the previous image. A $5,000 goal makes $4,000 seem like some degree of failure. And if you started out with the hope of $5,000, you'd have a certain amount of stress about reaching that goal. The expression "comparison is the killer of joy," is at play here because we're comparing our reality to our fantasy.

Going on vacation for a week in Florida could be a wonderful experience. But if we were hoping desperately to go to Bali, it might be a disappointment.

The Tao of Maybe gives us power over the most important thing: our reactions. Since, as the parable illustrates, we cannot ever truly know what lies ahead, awareness of our emotional response is far more effective than trying to control outside forces. Outcomes will always be unpredictable, but the ability to find peace and make ourselves feel safe is a game changer in any circumstance.

We're not suggesting you assume that the "best" will always happen. That's absurd. But if the outcome is already uncertain, there is no advantage to imagining the worst case scenario. In fact, there may be a considerable disadvantage.

There was a controversial subatomic physics study observing the crystallized patterns of water by Japanese scientist, Masaru Emoto, in which he proposed that the power of thought can organize atoms in the universe.

His exercise indicated that loving thoughts created beautiful, symmetrical patterns, while angry, disruptive thoughts created patterns of chaos in the water molecules.

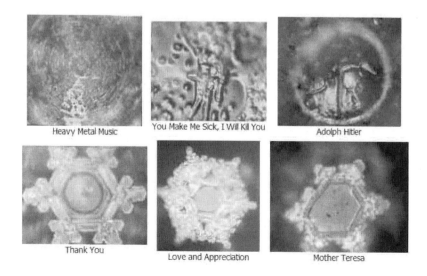

Heavy Metal Music   You Make Me Sick, I Will Kill You   Adolph Hitler

Thank You   Love and Appreciation   Mother Teresa

We know that the mind influences the cells in the body. You can watch a horror film with no physical threat present and manifest the very real, physical symptoms of a racing heartbeat, the release of adrenaline, and sweaty palms.

If 'maybe' still seems like the absence of 'hope' for the good stuff, consider what also doesn't exist… fear of the bad stuff. Trying to manifest the outcome we want could lead to satisfaction. But there are two other possible outcomes, which are negative:

1. The universe doesn't give us what we wanted, creating disappointment, and thereby putting out a negative vibration which affects our relationships and the energy we project, or

2. We get what we wanted, only to find that it doesn't bring us happiness after all, or worse… causes pain and suffering.

We really, really want that cute little apartment and jump through hoops to get it, only to move in and find out the neighbors practice drums until 3 a.m. Oops.

"SAMSARA
IS THE MIND TURNED OUTWARDLY,
LOST IN ITS PROJECTIONS.
NIRVANA
IS THE MIND TURMED INWARDLY,
RECOGNIZING ITS TRUE NATURE."

~ Sogyal Rinpoche

Maybe Exercise 5: Reverse Engineer It

Why do you want what you want?

This exercise is an homage to Simon Sinek's book for entrepreneurs, *Finding Your Why*. He discovered that businesses that knew why they were interested in selling a certain project were more successful. And the "why" couldn't just be to make money. It had to fill an existential or emotional need in the employee and consumer. We've applied that same logic to finding out why you want what you want. You may be surprised that the big car you want is really just a way to get your parents' or friends' respect as adults. Explore why you want the outcome you do. Don't edit yourself. (It may feel embarrassing, but who cares? You aren't sharing it with anyone, and you will learn about yourself in the process.)

1. What do you want?

2. Why do you want it? i.e.: what is the end result you want to achieve?

3. What is your motivation?

4. How will you feel when you have achieved your desired result?

An entry might look something like this:

1. Want: I want to lose 5 pounds.

2. Why: to fit into my skinny jeans.

3. Motivation: to look more attractive.

4. How I will feel: better about my body.

So you really want to feel better about your body. Let's work backwards. Your motivation is to look more attractive. You think it's by way of fitting into your skinny jeans.

Do you need to lose weight to do that? Maybe. But if you're at a healthy weight, dieting may not be the best answer and certainly isn't fun. So even if you achieve losing 5 pounds, you might not achieve the happiness you thought it would bring. What about this possibility: Through the years, your shape has changed. What if you look for jeans that are better suited for your shape?   You might feel better (the result you wanted) without unhealthy dieting.

You can then take it further with your new want.

1.   Want: I want to feel better about my body.

2.   Why: to rid myself of a negative body image.

3.   Motivation: emotional well being.

4.   How I will feel: I will feel lovable and worthy.

We don't really think that losing five pounds will make us feel more love. Don't we all know people who may not meet societal standards of beauty and yet radiate and receive love? We know that five pounds of body fat isn't linked to an idea as large and beautiful as self-love. But this is how the human psyche works. We make connections in our minds to some outside factors to blame for our displeasure. This is what happens when we ascribe goals without exploring root causes.

That is a prison of our own making that sends us down the road of constantly working on outside goals. When we abstract out our "real" goals, we may very well find that what we want is love or respect. This frees us up to look at all of the ways that we might increase love in our lives right now with friends, family, volunteering, work, therapy, and self-love.

If we decide we still want to lose weight, we can do it for reasons that expand our love for our body such as health, self-care, and feeling lighter, more energetic, and more comfortable. These are very likely outcomes, (whereas feeling lovable is not) and a better way to set ourselves up for success.

What we give our attention to becomes stronger, so it takes discipline to avoid focusing on the unwanted emotions in life. Making decisions from a place of anger, frustration or sorrow is almost always a losing proposition.

Chapter 6. What Are We Letting Go Of?

Maybe is the experience of weightlessness when we give the Universe the burden of our worries, and relax into the unknown. Alan Watts gave a brilliant lecture, (poeticized in "Waiting for Magic"), in which he explains this concept:

(excerpt by Alan Watts)

When you are silent it speaks, when you speak, it is silent.
The great gate is wide open, and nobody is obstructing it.
Now is where it's at.
It's where it's all going and where it all came from.
The whole thing is in the waiting.
There is nothing to do but wait.

The minute you try to hurry it, that introduces the one thing that stops it.

The miracle is happening all the time, but you can't see it when you're trying to get it, and you can still less see it when you're trying to get it fast.

So there is no alternative but to get to the point of you can't get it at all... then you start to be real.

What Watts captures so movingly is that our ideas, thoughts, and hopes are a 'net designed for catching water.' In other words, control is an illusion.

We can invite more calm, content happiness into our lives by doing less: by letting go of preference, trusting in what's to come, and leaning into curiosity.

If we believe the Maybe parable—that we can't know for sure what the best outcome is—then letting go of our preference for the outcome is the rational choice.

So how do we let go of the useless net of hope? How do we get to the point where we accept what happens as what IS, without positive or negative association?

First, we must agree with the Principles of Maybe...

1. Hope and fear both cause pain and suffering.

2. Control is an illusion.

3. Desperation takes us off our path.

IF SO, THEN:

Investing thoughts and energy on a future we cannot control is fruitless and detrimental for our mental and physical health.

AND THEREFORE:

4. True power is in the mastery of letting go of attachment to outcome.

Letting go should be the easiest thing in the world. It shouldn't require effort to NOT hold something, but it does. We have all sorts of creative methods of resistance. One of those is clinging to the cycle of *samsara* ("cyclic change" or "wandering").

We build emotional connections to past experiences. In Hindi, these are called cycles of *samsara*—the beginningless and endless cycle of birth, death, and rebirth; bringing pleasure and pain—and they can hold great power over our emotional state.

If you ever feel an emotion to an unfolding event that doesn't seem rational, you may be feeling the emotional connection to a past experience and not even know it.

When a current situation causes us to relive an unpleasant *samsara*, we want to run the other way to resist the emotions that surface. But we can't run away from our own minds.

Here is a very specific example of a personal *samsara*. A few years ago, while I was enjoying that exciting new relationship energy with a partner, he noticed that I was resistant to a particular touch. Although our sexual dynamics were very positive, in this one instance I would pull away, saying it was physically painful. The odd thing was that in his experience, this wasn't a common reaction for most women. I had assumed all my life that it was normal. This new perspective was very unexpected.

At the time, I didn't know about *samsara*, but something told me there was something beneath the surface. Instead of pushing the thoughts down, I allowed them to come up and simply observed what I was feeling. I was allowing a *samsara* to surface.

A few days later, it hit me like a cold splash of water in the face. I realized I had been molested at the age of seven by a male babysitter. I had always remembered that my 16-year-old neighbor made me feel weird by asking if he could play doctor with me. But in my revisionist story, I went to my room, closed the door, propped a chair under the knob, and curled up with my Pink Panther stuffed animal. And that was it.

I had NO recollection of him actually touching me until dozens of years later. Once acknowledged, I was capable of emotionally healing and removing the physical discomfort of what should have been pleasure.

Samsaras hold on to things that don't serve us. There are other, more subtle ways that we resist letting go. But it's an interesting exercise to ask ourselves what's really going on internally when we experience fear or anxiety. Often, if we're honest, we have the ability to let go of what hurts us, either on our own or with the help of a compassionate therapist.

We talk a lot about letting go in *The Tao of Maybe:* Letting go of attachment to an outcome, letting go of stressful thoughts, letting go of our old neural pathways.

That leaves empty space. And humans are remarkably good at filling up empty space with things. Move from a home with a small closet (which worked just fine) into a home with a big closet, and it will be filled in a week.

So when you let go of something, you might feel compelled to fill it with something else. Give up cigarettes, take up chewing gum. Leave a relationship, set up a dating profile.

Avoiding fear and sadness often leads to reaching for a vice to fill the space. A drink, a companion, food, video games. None of these is necessarily bad, but if they are an escape from thoughts and feelings, they are going to keep you from moving forward.

This is where self soothing comes in: Instead of turning away from uncomfortable feelings, relaxing into the discomfort. I like to imagine my inner child feeling the ugly feelings and me petting her hair or back to keep her soothed while she feels the uncomfortable feelings.

There is no way to get past something other than to go through it. Let it hurt until it doesn't hurt anymore. Let the fear seep in and observe it. And watch it eventually pass.

"Try not to resist the changes that come your way. Instead, let life live through you. And do not worry that your life is turned upside down. How do you know that the side you're used to is better than the one to come?"

~ Rumi

Maybe Exercise 6: Open Palm It

If you find it beyond your mortal means to let something go, turn to a bigger power. Let the Universe (or God, or whatever being or power or energy aligns with your beliefs) literally take it off your hands.

Author, Tosha Silver (*Outrageous Openness*), has a simple and effective method for doing this called "Open Palming" it.

Close your eyes.

Imagine your worry as an object. A rock, a handful of jelly, a hat. Whatever.

Imagine you are holding it in your hands.

Now hold your hands out for someone/thing to take it. Pass it on to the world, almost as a gift.

Say, "I've done all I can with this. It's yours now. Please take care of it."

Now it's not yours anymore. That worry simply doesn't belong to you.

Another tactic is a rather simple and funny one with surprising results. The next time you're trying to quiet your mind and pesky clouds of thoughts keep wafting in, say to yourself, "I wonder what my next thought will be."

It's an odd little moment. Almost like how a good comeback shuts down a comedian, it befuddles your mind. You may need to repeat it two or three times, but most often it stuns your inner dialogue just long enough to work!

Chapter 7. The Neuroscience of Your Thoughts

During his well-loved TED Talk about the human experience, Jeff Lieberman, an MIT-trained scientist, talks about the convergence of science and spirituality. He points out that humans belong to the only species that has "the power of prediction."

We alone anticipate events we have never before encountered. This is different from the way an animal learns patterns or acts on instincts when faced with danger or opportunity. Unlike animals, who base their actions on experience and genetic coding, we act on imaginary suppositions. Humans aren't born with this trait, we learn it.

If you've ever observed toddlers at play, you've seen how they live in the very real world of the emotions and sensations of the present. They don't think about what's next. A two-year-old building a sand castle isn't thinking; "Yikes, my mom is going to make me take a bath after this," or, "In about an hour I'm going to need a nap or a snack, " or, "High tide is duc in two hours."

So, if we aren't born with this as babies, when and where do we learn it? Could we unlearn that behavior? And would we want to?

This perpetual practice of anticipation causes us anxiety. It's so common and universal, we even have several ways to talk about it in the English language. The origin of the expression "waiting for the other shoe to drop" illustrates this perfectly:

> **A hotel guest was warned to be quiet because the guest in the room next to his was a light sleeper. As he undressed for bed, he forgot and dropped one shoe which awakened the other guest. He managed to get the other shoe off in silence, and went to sleep. An hour later, he heard a pounding on the wall and a shout: "When are you going to drop the other shoe?" Thus the term "waiting for the other shoe to drop." (Urban Dictionary)**

We get the joke immediately. And yet it's so strange because we are keeping ourselves awake worrying about something that we imagine is going to happen but doesn't.

This isn't to say we should never anticipate a potential outcome. Planning makes our lives easier and safer in many ways. Having a "rainy day" fund helps when the washing machine breaks, and checking the weather app before leaving the house prompts us to grab an umbrella. But as a society, we've developed a compulsion toward it as a way to defend ourselves from all the bad things happening in our heads, and we've lost the ability to balance it in moderation.

Imagine what would happen if we stopped letting our future control our present. Imagine letting go of our attachment to what we want, in exchange for appreciating what IS. Change is a constant, and we benefit from learning to embrace rather than resist it.

In the psychology abstract, "Twelve Potential Benefits of Living More Creatively," R. Richards says that remaining "dynamic" is one of those benefits:

> [C]omplete biological regularity can be lethal. Life is about infinite variation. Accepting this, we can be more in harmony, both within ourselves and the world, more open to change and surprise, and more alive.
> (Everyday Creativity)

The Story of Daniel:

Daniel had found the love of his life, Leesa. They got married, and Daniel set his mind on being a good partner and provider.

The couple's dream was to live in New York City, but rents were out of reach for the entry-level jobs of recent grads. With neither a suitable apartment nor a steady income, they were hesitant to start a family just yet. Daniel commuted to the City from a more affordable suburb.

After a year, things turned around. Daniel got a promotion and they could finally afford an apartment in the City and start planning for a baby. Soon after, Leesa was pregnant with their first child. Their lives were rich with beginnings and promise. A growing belly was the sign of their dreams coming true. All was going according to plan.

And then the most joyful time suddenly became their worst nightmare. Leesa lost the baby in a very late term miscarriage.

Their charmed life felt cursed. His perfect plan was obliterated.

In the days after the news, they couldn't think about the future. The only plan they could focus on for the moment, was a funeral.

They arranged for a small, private ceremony to bury their unborn child. The ceremony landed on a Tuesday morning. Daniel would need to take a personal day from work...

In the World Trade Center.

On Tuesday, September 11, 2001.

The death of his child may very well have saved Daniel's life.

If we track the emotions we feel as we hear Daniel's story, we might feel happiness for them or envy by way of comparison when everything is going great, then shock, sadness, grief, and fear that such a thing could happen to us.

The fear stage is very powerful. And while there, we jump to our worst outcome, paralyzed by the notion that we have no idea what the Universe has in store for us. We <u>hate</u> that. And we're afraid of it. That fear takes different forms. But many of them aren't real.

Robert Plutchik's Emotion Wheel

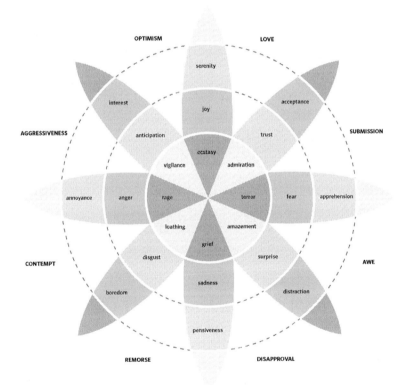

Robert Plutchik, who wrote extensively about emotions and evolution, created this emotion wheel and went on to propose that eight defense mechanisms were manifestations of the eight core emotions at the center of his wheel. (Notice "terror" is a core emotion.) Four of these common defense mechanisms look an awful lot like the kind of thinking we engage in when we are focused on an outcome we want or don't want.

DEFENSE MECHANISMS:

Wishful thinking

Projection

Fantasy

Paranoia

Emotions can certainly run the show for us. Many lucrative industries have capitalized on our desire to manage our anxieties about the future: insurance, palm reading, financial planning, religion, astrology, anti-aging products. When speculating about the future, we engage in the defense mechanisms of wishful thinking, projection, fantasy and paranoia. We accept past projections and forecasts because we imagine that forewarned is forearmed.

But is it?

Although it gives us comfort to show up prepared for life, what we are actually prepared for is only informed by the past. And there are no guarantees that the past will repeat itself. Very clear evidence of this came up as soon as Katherine and I started talking about the Daniel story.

When we discussed including Daniel and Leesa's story in our book, we found it fascinating that both of us felt strong, emotional responses to the story… for wildly different reasons. For me, this story is about 9/11. The grief and fear resonate with the nation's tragedy for intensely personal reasons. I lost my mom in the Twin Towers that day. However, for Kathy, the fear is about the loss of a child, again, for intensely personal reasons. It has been her greatest fear since she gave birth to her firstborn, perhaps because her mother had seven miscarriages before Kathy was born, and two after, and she was the only child to survive. Kathy can't even say "I have three healthy children" without immediately touching wood. If anxiety can be passed in utero, she got it.

We were both having emotional responses about our past experiences.

Though we know intellectually that Daniel's story isn't ours, irrational fears tend to take over. When I'm in a large confined public building, I imagine the chaos of a terrorist attack. Kathy feels the *samsara* of pregnancy fears because of her mother's miscarriages and one of her own.

In an effort to make meaning, we tell ourselves stories and we make things either "good" or "bad," when the truth is, they are neither. And both. We project our own past conditioning onto the future in a way that feels real, but isn't. What we think we know "for sure," just isn't necessarily true. And to be happier, we need to make friends with uncertainty. Even if our emotions are very compelling.

Neuroscientists term these strong, compelling emotions as "sticky," because they attach meaning to events. They form memories and habits. But because they are sticky, by definition, emotions are not detached. And as Tao and almost every other philosophy will tell you, attachment causes pain. In fact, Buddha said that all human suffering could be traced back to attachment: to fear and desire.

Fear and desire are very close cousins. Desire creates the fear that you won't have a good outcome. As Deepak Chopra explains in *Super Brain*, "Too intense a desire for success leads to stronger fears of failure, and if fear rises, it can create failure. The instinctive brain traps us between wanting something too much and not getting it at all," (116).

Fear creates <u>desire</u> (to avoid a bad outcome).

<u>Desire</u> creates <u>fear</u> (of not having a good outcome).

Fear and desire depend upon each other.

This black and white thinking isn't something we've done wrong. It's biologically predetermined. In the early development of man, in a constantly changing and ever hostile environment, we needed to be able to determine quickly whether a situation (or a berry) was good or bad. And while that upped our chances for survival then, it's getting us into trouble now because those fight or flight scenarios are happening constantly in our minds—and they are largely hypothetical.

But luckily, and very tellingly, our brains are moving beyond and away from the reactive fight or flight thinking that can be so uncomfortable and counterproductive to our emotional well-being, and evolving towards Maybe Thinking.

We can track the progression and adaptation of the human brain. First came the brain stem, also known as the reptilian brain. This is the part of the brain that urges us to act on our instincts for survival, fear, and desire. It is the panicked part of our brains that either wants or fears something beyond reason. It is where the Freudian *id* resides. Notice that this fight or flight mode causes every organism and every species an inordinate amount of biological stress. The Hairy Frog breaks its own toe bones and ejects them out of its feet like claws in an effort to repel predators; the Iberian ribbed newt breaks its own ribs through its skin to stab its predators. Reptiles have that reptilian brain, because their daily lives are still very much about survival. Life or death is still their main focus. But such extreme physical responses are only meant to be short term solutions from a biological perspective. Frogs and newts heal quickly and don't live that long.

Humans, however, live longer lives with much fewer instances of life and death threats. Biologically, we shouldn't need to engage our fight or flight responses thousands of times in our life or in our day. But we do. We make up reasons to engage those responses. Every time we feel that shoe hovering mid-air, we launch those biological systems.

Next on the evolutionary path came the limbic brain. This is the part of the brain that houses emotion and memories-- "I remember I liked that berry; it gave me pleasure, and I am going to eat it again." Emotions can be strong allies in our decision-making. In fact, studies have shown that in brain trauma victims, those patients who sustained damage to the emotion centers were suddenly rendered incapable of making decisions. Becoming aware of the emotions we are feeling is essential to personal growth and understanding our position in any given situation. We ignore our feelings at our own peril. But while it is important to recognize our triggers and reactions, (thank you, therapy), it is not necessary to act on them. In fact, very often it's most advantageous to find stillness.

There are excellent examples from nature of "life or death" situations resulting in better, less traumatic outcomes because the prey or victim literally did nothing. It's called "tonic immobility," "apparent death," or "playing dead." The opossum is most famous for the defense, but many animals use this strategy. It buys them time. They feel the emotional surge of fight or flight, and promptly shut down. The leaf frog even emits noxious "decomposition" fumes and fluids, though it is not dying, in order to make its fake death seem especially convincing.

Burmeister's leaf frog playing dead

Obviously shutting down and playing dead, isn't always available to us. But you can suspend your frenzied action or reaction. Every adult we know was taught the Stop, Drop, and Roll drill in response to fire as a child because running around just fans the flames.

Although animals react instantly on instinct as an automatic defense, with practice you can make a conscious choice to act or not, to feel peace, to refuse to fight or to take flight, all thanks to our brain's latest development: the Neocortex.

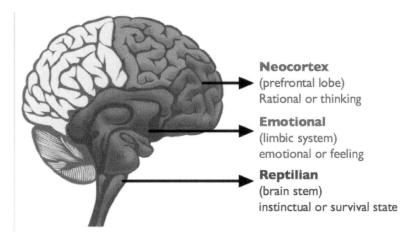

Neocortex
(prefrontal lobe)
Rational or thinking

Emotional
(limbic system)
emotional or feeling

Reptilian
(brain stem)
instinctual or survival state

The last to develop, the Neocortex, is the part of the brain where free will and intellect reign. It is the only part of the brain in which detachment thinking has a chance. It's interesting to note that you must be an evolved human being in order to access Maybe Thinking. Evolving toward a less reactive state is what our species needs for survival, health, and happiness. It is literally more evolved.

This is why Katherine and I started having Maybe conversations during carpool to writing group every Monday night. Our desire to jump mentally to the destination (worst or best case scenario) rather than to appreciate the vagaries of our present stage of the journey is an instinct. The science of our brains is wired (and chemically fitted for survival codes) for likely outcomes.

However, the definition of "likely outcomes" no longer applies to our complicated and subtle world. And it certainly does not apply to the nuances of adult relationships or allow us to make rational decisions under stress or when we feel threatened. Finally, it doesn't allow us the choice to simply be still and at peace until the way is made clear.

Brain evolution

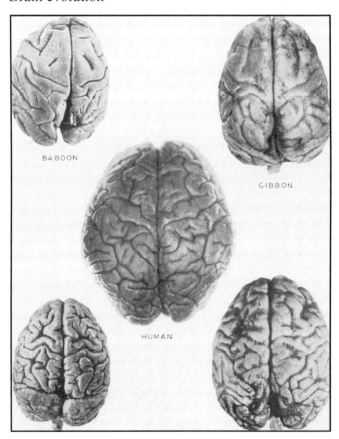

We can see, as it evolves, our neocortex is getting groovier. The shape of our brains has actually changed. Luckily, so too can the behavior of our brains.

"You cannot suffer the past or future because they do not exist. What you are suffering is your memory and your imagination."

~ Sadhguru

Maybe Exercise 7: Stop, Drop & Roll

Remember that assembly they taught at school - how to save ourselves if we ever caught on fire? Well, our brains are on fire every day, so let's put it to practice for non-attachment.

STOP - the behavior.

DROP - what you can (and should).

ROLL - with what's to come.

1. Stop-

When you feel a negative, spiraling feeling— worry, fear, stress, loneliness, despair—take a moment and stop (mentally, and sometimes physically) what you're doing. OBSERVE it, so you can begin to recognize part of the neuroplasticity cycle.

The thought is in your head; the feeling is in your body. Address both of them. Relaxing your body is a good place to start relaxing the mind. The next time you feel anxiety, take notice of your posture. Are your shoulders hiked up to your ears? Is your jaw clenched? Are your knuckles white? Is your stomach queasy? Do you feel the emotion in your throat, your back, your heart, your belly? These are signs that you are in fear.

Get curious and notice the bodily sensation. No judgment. Just observation.

You want to stop the thought from taking over, but that doesn't mean pretending it doesn't exist. Stopping your current thought and action is the first part of changing the bad habit and forming a new one.

2. Drop-

Once you've recognized the difference between a productive thought and an emotional reaction, DROP what you don't need. This is the "make a choice" part of the neuroplasticity cycle.

Don't confuse rational, action-oriented thoughts with stress-producing emotions. Productive thoughts will lead you to take reasonable actions to rectify a situation. If there is something you can do to improve the situation—most often, there is—then do so. If you're lonely, you might call a friend or attend a community event. If money is tight, you might apply for a new job, or see where you can trim your expenses. If you're running late for an appointment, you might ask a neighbor to get the kids to school to free up an extra 10 minutes. Looking for a job, in and of itself, does not cause stress. Reading a job post, writing a cover letter, hitting send—these are tasks which do not elicit an emotional attachment. Anticipation of the outcome does.

So after you've hit "send," mark your calendar to remind you of a day to follow up, then be done with it. Drop it.

Letting go of the unwanted thought is hard. Psychiatrist, Heidi Grant Halvorson suggests, "Blocking out (or "suppressing") a thought is challenging, because a blocked thought tends to rebound—in other words, it can come back later with a vengeance once you've let your guard down. The most well-known account of why rebounding happens comes from ironic monitoring theory. The idea is that, while you are blocking out a thought (for instance, trying to rid yourself of thoughts of "white bears"), part of your brain is actively searching for any thoughts of white bears so it can immediately shut them down. That search creates an ironic effect—it makes white bear thoughts more accessible, so that once you let your guard down and stop blocking, the thoughts come rushing back. Now all you can think about is white bears."

Instead, acknowledge it as its own independent entity. You cannot deny its existence. So let it be. Let it pass through you. Rather than "own it," stop seeing it as yours.

A lot of us get stuck at this very first step. "I can't," "The thought won't go away," "The feeling is bigger than I am."

This is all untrue.

You can.

It will.

And it's not.

Dr. Halvorson recommends two things. First acknowledge that it's not easy or even desirable to block a thought, so that you don't get frustrated with yourself. Just accept that you don't actually need the thought. Secondly, with persistent or recurring thoughts, come up with a plan. Decide that when this unwanted thought comes, you will direct your thoughts to another more positive thought to replace it. Since it's not neurologically possible to think of two things simultaneously, you need to choose a better thought to override the unwanted one.

Employ a replacement thought. Or perhaps have a "Maybe buddy" on hand - find a friend on this journey of letting go, whom you can call when you're having trouble with a thought. They can remind you that you don't need the thought, that it WILL pass. You can help each other create a better "replacement thought" for the times when you haven't planned ahead for them.

3. Roll-

When you've done what you can do, it's time to let go of the struggle. Watch with curiosity what the Universe brings you, and roll with the flow of what comes.

Chapter 8. Rewiring the Brain

What the Tao of Maybe is really aiming to do is break the habit of your thought patterns. And what is a habit? It's a repeated thought or action that's executed by the brain automatically, without consideration.

Habits are both behavioral and physical. In the 1960s Dr. Maxwell Maltz wrote a book, *Psycho-Cybernetics* describing how habits work. Maltz was a plastic surgeon who'd observed during his 1950s practice that his patients took at least 21 days to get used to the look of a new nose, or the feel of an amputation, etc. After doing his own personal experiments affirming that it also took him 21 days or more for an old mental image to dissolve and a new one to gel, he wrote his famous book. This predominantly anecdotal guide was so widely read, that it became common knowledge that it takes three weeks to form a habit.

Years later, Phillipa Lally and her research team decided to run a clinical study to get some real data, and after 12 weeks with 96 participants found his work to be largely correct with the caveat that 21 days was the strict minimum required.

> **On average, it takes more than two months before a new behavior becomes automatic — 66 days to be exact.**

To change the habit of our thoughts, we turn to neuroplasticity, which is responsible for our learning and memory. An ability to remap is the brain's creative response to an ever-changing environment. When we try to remember a new friend's favorite food because we are inviting them to dinner and want to please them, we are creating neural connections between that person and the food. How well that evening goes will strengthen the memory with an emotional connection (positive or negative) or weaken it if the evening was boring and uneventful. This is how we learn throughout our lives up until we die.

Every behavior that we learn can be phased out, and a better behavior can be put in its place. "Research has shown that cortical networks in the brain change, including synaptogenesis, neurogenesis, and programmed cell death, as a result of one's experience." (*Bjorklund & Lindwall, 2000*)

How We Rewire Our Brains.

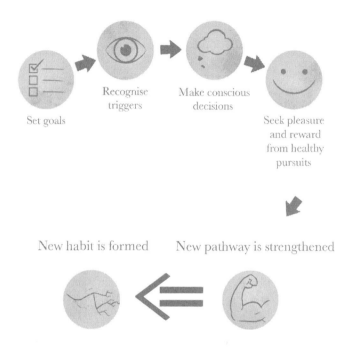

Set goals → Recognise triggers → Make conscious decisions → Seek pleasure and reward from healthy pursuits

New habit is formed   New pathway is strengthened

These connections in the neocortex change constantly. And what's very exciting is that by consciously re-directing our thoughts, we can choose to create new neural pathways with positive emotions. However, be aware that it requires a conscious choice. In the absence of a conscious re-wiring practice the brain will subconsciously and automatically default to known pathways. And based on the society we live in, those will most likely be carved out of fear.

In *Anatomy of Spirit,* spiritual and medical intuitive Caroline Myss observes:

"Every choice we make, motivated by either faith or fear, directs our spirit. If a person's spirit is impelled by fear, then fear returns to her energy field and to her body. If she directs her spirit in faith, however, then grace returns to her energy field, and her biological system thrives."

Tara Brach, meditation guru and author of *Radical Acceptance*, locates the sources of unhappiness and worry to "if-only mind." This is thinking that says if only circumstances were different, (I was richer, skinnier, more attractive, smarter), my life would be better. "If only" also takes the form of wishing other people were different, or we were different. And she states quite unequivocally, "We are regularly wrong in what we think will help us. We are tensed against the future, in Worrier Pose." Problem mode creates negativity bias - not a good strategy for intimacy, for trust, for our bodies, or for enjoying life.

It's what happens when we base our happiness on external conditions. In Sanskrit this is called *preya* and it is a set-up for suffering because life and conditions will always change. Mortality is the ultimate proof of that.

"Maybe Thinking" is finding *sukha*, which is Sanskrit for unconditional happiness—acknowledging that this moment right now is enough. We are happy for no reason. This is much more satisfying than happiness based on external things or events, and the best part is that you needn't wait for something to come to get it. It's accessible to you in every moment. According to Brach,

- It's saying, "We are whole." Instead of, "Something's missing."
- It's saying, "We are okay." Instead of, "Something's wrong."

The French were onto something with the expression *"Que sera, sera"* (Whatever will be will be). That thinking allows us to live in the now. "It is the wisdom of true happiness" according to Brach.

You may think, yeah right. If it were that easy to stop worrying, we'd all do it. But the truth is, you just have to start a new habit. It won't happen the first or even 13th time that extra bill comes in that you don't have the funds for, or you're bound to miss your flight, or your kid isn't doing well in school. But it will happen if you keep at it.

When I first started this practice, it wasn't easy. My brain went down those worrisome neural pathways like they always had. I had to literally engage in mini conversations with myself in my head:

Me: I'm worried about x.

Maybe Me: You're not supposed to worry.

Me: Yeah, but-

Maybe Me: Have you done everything you can do to avoid/prepare/remedy the situation?

Me: Well, yeah.

Maybe Me: If you worry about it, will it be less likely to happen?

Me: Well, no.

Maybe Me: Okay then, let's do one of those open palming exercises and let the Universe handle it.

Me: Okayyyyy.

And wouldn't you know it, that eventually became habit. Now it's second nature to arrive at the conclusion that the Universe will handle it. My stress rarely flares up and my default mode has become "maybe."

It's imperative to work on breaking our old thought habits because the alternative is simply unacceptable.

If we continually fight what is happening to us, we create resistance, and resistance to life creates stress. The brain doesn't know the difference between *good* and *bad*. It simply knows the *what*. It learns whatever thoughts, actions and habits are repeated—both helpful and unhelpful (National Institute for the Clinical Application of Behavioral Medicine). Obsessively worrying about the same thing over and over makes the neurons fire in a familiar pattern that becomes habit and forms links in the brain that literally make us stuck in that rut.

Instead we want to break up the patterns of worry to alleviate stress and all its nasty side effects.

"What happens instead when we let go of a feeling? The energy behind the feeling is instantly surrendered and the net effect is decompression. We feel happier, more loving, and more easygoing." (Letting Go, 14-15, Hawkins)

When we become neutral about the future rather than being fearful or optimistic—pessimism or optimism—we allow ourselves to be <u>curious</u>. The more we practice it, the easier it gets, because we are literally rewiring our brains.

Maybe proposes that pathway to rewiring. It starts with self-awareness: taking stock of feelings as they arise; neither judging nor suppressing them, simply observing them for the data they provide; breathing—neither acting, nor reacting; and finally, choosing a different thought that is no more or less true than the negative one.

This process may sound deceptively simple. Because it IS simple… but not easy (at first, anyway). You've been thinking the same way for decades. It's going to take a little practice to think differently. Over time it can become second nature and we need nothing more than the desire to shift our thinking to start that path.

You can absolutely do it.

"If you want a new outcome,
you will have to break the
habit of being yourself, and
reinvent a new self."

~ Dr. Joe Dispenza

Maybe Exercise 8: Keep Calm and Carry On

One of the biggest hurdles of "letting go" is our lack of control of our own thoughts. We find ourselves prisoners of our minds. Try not thinking about a pink elephant for the next 30 seconds and it's pretty hard not to have that elephant creep back into your consciousness over and over again. It can feel like we have no say in what our minds conjure up.

Thoughts are real. They DO exist. And to pretend that they don't is futile, a waste of time, and even destructive. But it's important to make the distinction that they are not "us."

A useful tool used by Julia Cameron (*The Artist's Way*) is to write what she calls morning pages. This is the basic practice of journaling with very specific parameters. Do it first thing in the morning and write exactly three pages.

It's just meant to be stream of consciousness, with the intent to empty our minds of the silly little worries banging around in our brains from the moment we wake up. The goal is not to create a list of problems to solve, in fact, she urges her students to never even go back and look at the pages. Many of her students consider this an essential part of their day.

Chapter 9. Bypassing Your Brain

A lot of the discussion in this book is centered around our reactions to relationships and situations that cause us stress or anxiety—the bad things. But what about the stress and anxiety we feel just by being faced with a tough decision? Having two great job offers isn't a bad thing, but man can we spin ourselves in a tizzy trying to figure out which is the "right" one to take. We often call this a "good problem," but it's a problem nonetheless because it presents stress.

So how can we take anxiety out of the decision making process?

There are loads of methods to making a decision—researching details, making lists of pros and cons, polling your friends. But even with all that work done, often we still sit staring at two or more options and feeling lost for what to choose.

In fact, some research shows that the longer we contemplate a decision the farther we get from feeling certain about the conclusion. That's because the first answer that pops in our heads is usually the best one for us. That first answer comes from a feeling, before our thinking brain has a chance to pile on a shroud of complications and doubt. Essentially, we already know what we "want" before we "think" about it, and that's our **intuition**.

Intuition is a complex phenomena. In terms of neurology, intuition can be explained through the activity of the amygdala, which is responsible for processing emotions and triggering the fight or flight response. Some research has found chemical reactions occur in the body during a reported intuitive experience. Although the Western world hasn't defined intuition as a concrete science, most of us know it's as real as the wind—you can't see it, but you can feel it.

Somatic knowledge (of the body, as distinguished from the mind, soul, psyche; corporeal; physical) is the body's awareness that involves senses and perceptions. It's your body's communication to your brain. In other words, your body knows things before your brain thinks it.

We can notice somatic reactions in everyday reactions like raising our shoulders or clenching our jaws, or more habitual reactions like a tic—tapping our feet, biting our nails. And what about that sinking feeling in your stomach when you get bad news?

The expression "gut feeling" means exactly that—a feeling or idea that comes from our intestinal tract.

The gut-brain-gut communication network is part of the interoceptive circuits which enable the brain to sense and interpret the physiological condition in the body and regulate its autonomic and mental activity accordingly (*National Library of Medicine, 2022 - Peter Holzer*).

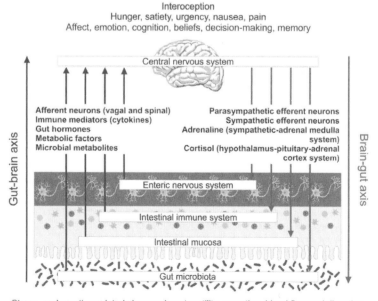

Interoception
Hunger, satiety, urgency, nausea, pain
Affect, emotion, cognition, beliefs, decision-making, memory

Central nervous system

Afferent neurons (vagal and spinal)
Immune mediators (cytokines)
Gut hormones
Metabolic factors
Microbial metabolites

Parasympathetic efferent neurons
Sympathetic efferent neurons
Adrenaline (sympathetic-adrenal medulla system)
Cortisol (hypothalamus-pituitary-adrenal cortex system)

Gut-brain axis

Brain-gut axis

Enteric nervous system

Intestinal immune system

Intestinal mucosa

Gut microbiota

Stress- and emotion-related changes in gut motility, secretion, blood flow and digestion

If we look at history, some cultures dating back to ancient Mayans and beyond believed the brain in our head is the "little brain," in charge of motor skills and keeping the body alive. But the "big brain," in charge of feelings and decisions, is actually in our gut.

If we look at science, this idea isn't so farfetched. Consider the convergence of three things:

1.   There are more bacteria in your gut than there are grains of sand on the earth or stars in the sky.

2.   Bacteria have been on earth for over 3 billion years. That's at least a cool bill or two before humans showed up.

3.   It's a widely considered theory that living beings have ancestral knowledge.

Ergo, your gut biome may contain billions of years of wisdom. It's not that big of a stretch when you look at how many millennia bacteria have survived, while thousands of other living things have gone extinct.

There is much excitement in scientific communities about the research of inherited knowledge—that is to say, information that a living being obtains through genetics. In one study (Princeton University, 2020 - Coleen Murphy), researchers found that roundworms had the ability to transmit information to future generations through cells in the nervous system. If that is true, the same is likely for one of our oldest living organisms: bacteria. And we just happen to be walking around with billions of them in our bellies.

So instead of thinking of yourself as a single human walking around the world with ideas and thoughts created all by you, think of a human as a walking ecosystem with billions of years of data.

Of course, much of this is exploratory theory. Perhaps it's coincidence, or confirmation bias, or God, or something else entirely. But for generations, we've been noticing the hair standing up on the back of our necks, "chills," or an inexplicable feeling to choose something out of our norm.

Perhaps having a "gut feeling" isn't magical or supernatural. It's your gut biome collaborating to send you information that the brain doesn't see.

So how do you identify intuition? And how can you tell it apart from needless worrying?

A thought that comes from intuition:

- Is short and uncomplicated—in fact it is almost always singular in idea.

- Does not usually have any words attached to it.

- Can be a feeling that comes from either a physical or emotional origin.

- Can sometimes be seen as a color, shape, or symbol.

- Is usually repetitive, or keeps coming back.

- Is light and subtle in content, a whisper as opposed to a shout.

- Is free from emotion, as in not angry or scared or euphoric, just *right*.

Intuition will either draw you to, or repel you from, something. Maybe it's a physical situation, maybe it's a decision you're considering. Your gut will give you a simple, clear feeling that is usually Yes or No, Go or Stop. You can generally feel a sense of either opening (a yes) or contracting (a no) when considering an option.

Listening to and acting on our intuition can strengthen it, like a muscle, so that your answers come more and more quickly and insistently.

How to Listen:

Think of your subconscious as your silent admin assistant, the keeper of the file cabinet and director of the comms facility. This "assistant" communicates with all the other parts of you, while having an encyclopedia of relevant, but arcane knowledge and constantly observing and taking notes about the outside world that you come into contact with.

Now pretend you can have a conversation with your intuition. Here's how it's going to go. You're going to ask a question about a decision you have to make. And this "assistant" is going to answer with one short, clear, uncomplicated response. It could be through a variety of senses, with a smell, a sound, a taste, a feeling on your skin, or deep within your organs.

But it will be a sensation of clarity, without questions or caveats or hesitation. You will feel closed or open. Growing or shrinking. Moving forward or stuck. It's easy to decipher if you're listening.

You might ask, what if I don't get any of that? It's possible that you just don't have or need intuition for this particular thing. We don't feel it all day every day. It would be too distracting to function. It could also mean there is not a strong answer, or that the situation is still evolving and your intuition needs a little more time. Maybe both jobs have equal but different appeal. Maybe the guy you're dating is fine—no red flags—but not reliving scenes from *The Notebook* either. Or maybe your intuition is telling you to do nothing and wait a bit. Sometimes doing nothing is also the right action.

Intuition usually shows up when it's important. And when it's needed. Chances are you can recall moments when you heard it and disregarded it, only to regret it later.

Intuition is that thing whispering to your brain. And your goal is to tune in and listen so you can hear it clearly and act on it whenever needed.

"FAITH REQUIRES FOLLOWING THE
POWER OF A WHISPER."

~ Shannon L. Alder

Maybe Exercise 9: Get Out of Your Own Way

Both building new neural pathways and getting in touch with your body's messages, relies on getting out of the rote actions we do everyday. If you do the same things in the same order, you will be living the same experience and having the same thoughts, without noticing much of anything.

1. Get out of your routine.

Change things up on the daily. Reorder your morning routing. Coffee BEFORE shower (or vice versa). Allow ten minutes to take a different route to work. Take yourself to dinner alone at a new restaurant. Journal a thought, but then respond to that thought with your non-dominant hand. This will also visually remind you of childlike writing which can help bring out curiosity and suspend judgment.

Another tool in *The Artist's Way* by Julia Cameron is to take yourself on a date once a week. Do something new, silly, frivolous.

2. Let your body do the talking.

In moments of decision making, become more aware of what's going on with your body. Get as calm as you can physically and mentally, and then focus on the issue at hand. Now notice what (and where in your body) you feel. Do your shoulders and jaws clench? Do your hands rub together? Does your stomach feel queasy? There are many areas and ways we can feel emotions in our bodies. Learn to tell the difference between nervous fear (a no) and nervous excitement (a yes). But as a rule of thumb:

> **Feeling open and / or leaning forward is a sign of an intuitive YES.**
>
> **Feeling tight and/ or a sense of retreating is a sign of a NO.**

This may seem obvious, but if you don't stop to notice it, you can easily miss what your intuition is telling you.

Let's say someone asks if you'd like to go on a trip. Imagine the trip as a physical object on the table in front of you. Do you feel the desire to lean in to inspect it or lean back and not engage with it? Are you fidgety (excited) or closed down (fearful)?

Need a little further help getting anxiety out of the way? Below are two techniques used to do just that. They can be done for a few minutes every day to build on a practice, or at specific times of anxiety.

Please note: these are exercises often used in conjunction with therapy, because they can bring up deep rooted emotions and trauma. If you begin to notice that you feel MORE anxious when doing them, please stop and only revisit with your mental health guide.

1. Tapping. Put your hands in front of you, palms facing toward you, and hook your thumbs together —creating a butterfly shape. Rest the heels of your hands in the center of your chest, allowing your fingers to rest on your collar bone. Now close your eyes and alternate tapping all four of your fingers on one hand and then the other in a moderate pace (roughly 1/2 second for each hand).

2. Rapid Eye Movement. This is easiest done with a friend, but eventually you should be able to do it on your own. With a friend, have them hold a finger, pen, or other object a few inches in front of your face and move the finger or object back and forth rapidly—about a foot or so in distance, three to four passes (side to side) per second. Do this for about 30 seconds. If you're doing it on your own, choose two visual points in front of you. It can be a few inches away or the other side of the room. Just be sure that the points are clear and fixed and easy targets to focus on. Then, do the same process of looking back and forth rapidly for about 30 seconds.

Is that Really *It*?!

Is it just that simple?

Maybe.

Although many disciplined seekers have achieved total and lasting "enlightenment," most of us take two steps forward and one step back on a journey toward inner peace. The less you try, the easier the path. There is no medal, no finish line, and no competition. You are the only player in this game you're trying to win.

It's important to remember that happiness is always within reach. It's the starting point and the ending point. We'll find it for moments and struggle to get back to it at others.

Happiness is what we knew as children, but have forgotten. It's what social programming has trained out of us. And to get back to it, we need simply to let go.

A father of a teen who had died a violent death was interviewed because of his surprisingly happy view of life in the aftermath. When asked why he wasn't angry or depressed, he simply asked, "Why would I want to be angry or sad? Neither will bring my son back, and living the rest of my life in grief doesn't sound like a life well-lived."

Each day. Each event. Each time something presents us with anxiety, or breaks our heart, or fills us with dread or worry… we must ask ourselves, "Is this thing worth giving away my peace?" It is truly our choice. And the only thing in this world we have control over: our reactions.

1. We can decide we want to (and know we have the ability to) be at peace.
2. We can let go of attachment—trade in fear and hope for trust and curiosity.
3. We can employ the practices in this book when those nagging thoughts threaten our peace, and rewire our brains for happiness.

The power of Maybe is in our hands. It always was. It always will be. The gate is wide open, with nothing standing in our way but ourselves.

"WHAT DAY IS IT?" ASKED POOH.
"IT'S TODAY." SQUEAKED PIGLET.
"MY FAVORITE DAY." SAID POOH.

~ A.A. Milne

Curated Maybe Stories

Stumbling Back to Consciousness

"Two weeks ago, Sunday, in the middle of the night, I tripped over the carpet in the bathroom and gave myself a concussion. I have headaches and some memory loss, but what I have gained far outweighs what I lost.

See, the trip to the hospital was the first day I hadn't had a drink in almost a year to the day. It is the first time I have been completely sober since the morning I found out Trump had been elected.

I had been sober for three months prior to the election. No therapist (and I've been) would diagnose me as an alcoholic, but when you realize a hospital stay is the only thing that keeps you from a drink... well, a diagnosis is not needed.

I think hitting the floor and being knocked out, literally knocked some sense into me, when I was again heading down such a destructive path, both to self and to those I love. Two weeks is both a short time and an eternity, but I am grateful."

~ Name withheld upon request

John's Life Sentence

The 1980's wasn't an easy time to be gay. Culturally, it was still not widely "accepted" and the AIDS epidemic was at its frightening apex. But being in New York City, was at least one of the areas of the country with a large, gay community.

For John, who worked at a well known cable network in Midtown, working with comforting friends was essential.

One morning in 1989, he went to his doctor's office for the results of some tests, and received the worst news he could have dreamt of. The news was grim. He indeed had AIDS, and also cancer. The doctor told him he had about two years to live and ought to go home and get his affairs in order.

John didn't have the capacity to go home and tell his loving partner that he was going to die in two years. He was at a loss for what to do and where to go, and as odd as it seemed, he wanted to go to the office. He knew that his friend, Sandy, would have a shoulder to cry on and a kind word to soothe him.

But after laying the heavy news on her, she responded quite differently than he had imagined.

She said, "You don't know and your doctor doesn't know how much time you have. You might only have a week. And even if he was right, that you definitely have two years to live... are you going to throw them away by spending those days feeling sorry for yourself? How dare you squander those two years."

Her words were harsh given his fragile emotional state, but she grabbed her purse and took him on a long meandering walk around the city. They walked and talked for hours.

Sandy insisted that she had the guarantee of two years no more than he did, and encouraged him to put the death sentence aside. She urged him instead to remember that the only promise any of us ever has is the current moment. And if that's all there is, there is no point worrying about how many future moments we might get.

They had stopped for lunch and when they stepped back out onto the street she turned her face up to the sunny sky, closed her eyes and smiled, and said, "It's such a beautiful day, John. This is as good as it gets."

And he got it. In that moment, he got what she meant. That the only moment that matters is the current one. And he vowed to embody that sentiment.

When Sandy passed, 12 years later, John would call to share his condolences. A call he made 10 years past his "expiry" date.

Sandy's talk that day may or may not have contributed to how long he would live, but it definitely made an impact on HOW he lived.

Bad Luck(y)

"After graduating college in the spring of 1989, I went out to Wyoming to be a camp counselor. On July 16th we had a camp outing. Camp bus wasn't big enough to transport kids and counselors so counselors had to drive separately. As luck would have it my car wouldn't start that day (started the day before and the day after when my parents went to retrieve it from camp). Because my car wasn't working I had to be a passenger in another vehicle. The driver was speeding on a gravel road and lost control. The car flipped several times and I was thrown 100 feet.

At a small hospital in Wyoming I was told I would never walk nor have children again. I broke my back at L1 vertebrae with initial total paralysis. My spinal cord was not severed so there was potential for improvement. I worked hard and after a year and a half of intense physical therapy, both inpatient and outpatient, I walked full time with the aid of canes and foot orthotics.

After graduating from Boston College Law School in 1992 I began working as an assistant district attorney in the Kings County District Attorney's Office in Brooklyn, NY. I met my husband while working as an ADA in Brooklyn and we defied the no children diagnosis by having three kids. I created an amazing life and family that probably only happened because of my injury and recovery.

Jump to the first week of March 2015. Bad news after bad news. My father was in the hospital with congenital heart failure and they had decided that he wasn't eligible for open heart surgery. The doctor expected my dad to live at least a year!?! My husband was dealing with a very difficult situation at work and we were considering hiring an attorney to try to ameliorate the situation. Snow, frigid weather and ice midweek. On Thursday March 5th my kids had no school and we got the call that we had a delayed opening the next day March 6th.

Given the awful week we were having, I sent everyone to bed and decided I would stay up to have another glass of wine, unwind and just enjoy the silence. I usually went to bed at the same time as my husband but not on this night. I was still at the kitchen table when I began to smell smoke. I was rushing around the kitchen (I always left my canes in the car) and found that the dryer was on fire. The laundry room was on the 1st floor next to the garage. I opened the garage door to grab the fire extinguisher which created a draft for the smoke which set the fire alarms off. My daughter came running down and I told her to go get my husband. We had an older fire extinguisher which had a metal pin that you pull out and insert back into the hole to get it to work. NOT easy to do when you are inches away from flames. My husband came down and went about getting the extinguisher to work while I yelled for the kids to sit by the front door until we put the fire out.

My husband got the extinguisher to work and put out the flames coming from underneath the dryer. I yelled to the kids that we got it, all was good and then yelled for them to get out when my husband opened the drum of the dryer to see flames raging.

My boys ran to the neighbors, my daughter helped me crawl out of the house, while my husband went to find the dog that we had let out of the house through the sliding back door. We watched the flames grow until they blew out the window and began to consume our house in front of our very eyes.

Make note of the fact that our lovely and bucolic town has only volunteer firefighters and not paid members. The volunteers abandoned their cars stuck in the snow to run to the station to get to us. But despite four fire companies responding, the water from the fire hose froze as they tried to put out the fire and the stars aligned to burn it down to the ground. Nothing was saving the house. Ultimately it had to be torn down because it was structurally unsound.

This fire was going to happen no matter what. The faulty Electrolux Dryer (unbeknownst to us) happened to catch fire at 10pm at night while I would normally have been in bed, were it not for the trying week and the snow days. If I had been asleep there is no way we would have all gotten out alive. The fire was that fast and furious.

We lost so much but we gained that much more. My children witnessed a town rally behind us and shower us with generosity. My husband left his job (they gave him severance) and he got a new job which allowed him to work from home. The fire put things in perspective and he realized that toxic colleagues and a stressful work environment are not worth it. Prior to the fire, he left before 7am and was rarely home before 7:30pm. My children went from seeing their dad about 10-15 hours a week to seeing him all of the time. Their relationship has grown tenfold. And we had an amazing insurance company that allowed us to rebuild a gorgeous new home, this time with an elevator to help me navigate the floors.

I am going to steal a quote from an essay my daughter wrote about the fire. "From the fire, I learned there is faith to be found in tragedy, light to be found in darkness. From the ruins around me, I learned that crumbling is often necessary. From my family, I learned that relationships grow with hardship. From myself, I learned that becoming resilient is painstaking, but that it is also my proudest accomplishment."

Break a Leg

"In 2004, I booked my first ever paying theatre gig, with "Paint Your Wagon" at the Geffen Playhouse under director Gil Cates. Just days later, frolicking on the sidewalk after a commercial audition, I rolled and sprained my ankle so badly it swelled to the size of a grapefruit. I stayed on the production for a week, but it became painfully clear I would never be able to dance, let alone walk, as the role required.

I withdrew from the production and pouted on the sofa as my ankle healed through November/December. Because I was no longer in the show, I was able to fly back east for Christmas ... where I took a long-delayed meeting with the director of my old summer music camp (Hartwick College Summer Music Festival & Institute, née NYSMC—New York State Music Camp).

Because of that face to face meeting, I was offered a full one-month position as their new "Instructor of Musical Theatre." And in that meeting, I decided to also teach classes in Acting and Filmmaking.

My four weeks there were such a success that immediately after the end of camp, she offered me the position of Assistant Camp Director.

I accepted, but then she was fired by the Hartwick camp!

Purely to show them they had erred, she opened a completely new summer music camp—NYSMF New York Summer Music Festival—and invited me to become a co-founder and co-director.

I took the title of Director of Communications + Director of the Writing & Acting Program. Until my departure in 2013, I taught up to four classes a day in acting, filmmaking, and original musical theatre, eventually producing over 20 student-written one act musicals and 100 short films.

All because I rolled my ankle.

ABOUT THE AUTHORS

Dr. Katherine Boutry

Katherine's work has always focused on helping people live their best, most creative lives. As Director of the Creativity Studies Lab and Chair of eleven departments in the Language Arts Division at West Los Angeles College, she launched the first Creativity Studies and Innovation certificate program at a community college in the State of California. She spearheaded the annual The Creative Edge Creativity Conference, a TED Talk-like event around creativity, now in its third year. She is author of *The West Guide to Writing* and several articles on the link between Creativity and Well-Being. Katherine has presented her work at the American Creativity Association, the League for Innovation, the Torrance Creativity Roundtable, the Knowledge, Innovation, and Entrepreneurship Conference and at the Creativity Expert Exchange sponsored by the Center for Creativity Studies at SUNY, Buffalo where she is working on her MS in Creativity and Change Leadership. She is a creativity coach and principal of Make Lemonade Creativity Consulting and is developing The Creativity App and The Tao of Maybe Podcast.

Katherine earned her PhD from Harvard University and taught there for ten years as a lecturer and Assistant Director of

Undergraduate Studies where she advised 350 students in making big life decisions. She left Harvard to become a staff writer on the television show Missing (Lifetime/Lionsgate) and The Haunting Hour, and recently optioned her original pilot The Virgins (about women and faith) to Sundance and Radar. She is head writer on a 52-episode television series, NYALA, for RTI in Cote d'Ivoire, Africa. While on hiatus, she created the MFA in Creative Writing at Mount Saint Mary's University. She was a Fulbright Scholar in the Czech Republic. She continues to blend writing and innovative teaching. She has lived and worked in Paris, the Czech Republic, Rome and London, has her motorcycle license, climbed the unrestored sections of the Great Wall of China, and summited Mount Kilimanjaro and Mount Salkantay with her three children, Maximilien, Penelope, and Lily. She lives and writes in Los Angeles, California.

Shelli Wright

Shelli is a NJ native, and Rutgers alumni. She's been an ad agency copywriter working on big brands (Samsung, Volkswagen, TJ Maxx, Taco Bell, UPS, Jeep, Fox Sports); a producer and choreographer of live theater (Six Flags theme parks, and Isle of Capri Casinos); an event producer (Austin City Limits, Special Olympics, Google events, and celebrity comedy fundraisers at The Hollywood Improv). She wrote and co-executive produced a pilot ("The Anea Show") for PBS, has sold and optioned features and TV pilots, as well as winning or placing in numerous screenplay competitions (Amazon Studios, Austin Film Fest, Second City, and Sundance Writer's Lab).

Her work with REALgirl empowerment programs led to starting a tampon company, TrueMoon, with educational outreach about the moon cycle. As founder and CEO, Shelli was invited to be a mentor in a transformational high security prison program.

Shelli has studied Taoism, Buddhism, Sikhism, Shinto and Kabbalah. She is a traveler of over 25 countries, a free-range parent of two, and a life learner.

A Few Additional Reading Suggestions…

Radical Acceptance, Tara Brach

The Seven Spiritual Laws of Success, Deepak Chopra

The Untethered Soul, Michael Singer

Breaking the Habit of Being You, Dr. Joe Dispenza

Outrageous Openness, Tosha Silver

You Can Heal Your Life, Louise Hay

The Artist's Way, Julia Cameron

The Big Leap, Gay Hendricks

The Anatomy of Spirit, Caroline Myss

The God of Happiness

One day a very sad human approached their God and asked, "Can you make me happy?"

The God replied, "Yes I can. I will make something happen that will give you eternal happiness. But you must pretend to be happy until then, so that by the time I grant it, you will be ready."

So they practiced being happy. They smiled and skipped and whistled and hugged people. They practiced faithfully for a year, then went to their God and said, "I've done what you asked. I practiced. Will you make the something happen that will give me eternal happiness, now?

And the God said, "Be patient a while longer, be patient. Keep practicing. It will be worth it."

They went on to practice for a year and another year and another year, and after five years, they went back to the God and said, "I've done what you asked. I've practiced, I've gotten really good. In fact, I'm quite an expert! Will you please make the something happen that will give me eternal happiness, NOW?"

The God replied, "Yes. You've done well," He paused. "I have done it now."

They became excited, "Will I see it when I get home? Will I meet someone on my way? What is it?"

And the God said,

"You already have it."

They looked around and felt their pockets. And then became confused, "Where?"

And the God said, "I have given you the power to create eternal happiness from within. You no longer need to seek outside yourself for it."

"What if it all works out…"

~ Jitterbug